CAREER

OPPORTUNITIES

in MAGAZINE

PUBLISHING

CAREER
OPPORTUNITIES
in MAGAZINE
PUBLISHING

THE ULTIMATE GUIDE TO
SUCCEEDING
IN THE BUSINESS

RALPH MONTI

SPECIAL INTEREST MEDIA
BLOOMFIELD, NEW JERSEY

Published by:

Special Interest Media
72 Hyde Road
Bloomfield, NJ 07003
Tel: (973) 338-4447
Fax: (973) 893-8078
e-mail: specint@intac.com

Publisher's Cataloging-in-Publication
Monti, Ralph.
Career opportunities in magazine publishing :
the ultimate guide to succeeding in the business /
Ralph Monti. -- 1st ed.
p. cm.
Preassigned LCCN: 98-96816
ISBN: 1-884490-16-6
1. Periodicals, Publishing of--Vocational
guidance. I. Title.

　　　　Z286.P4M66 1999　　　070.5'72'023
　　　　QBI98-1691

For school, group or bulk purchases, contact Special Interest Media.

Cover design: Ernie Parada
Book design: Norma Jean DeVico

ABOUT THE AUTHOR

Ralph Monti is currently President of Cherry Lane Magazines, LLC, a division of the Cherry Lane Music Group, one of the world's largest music publishers that specializes in music publishing, magazine publishing, sheet music, songbooks, CD-ROMS and multimedia. Monti has more than 20 years in magazine publishing management, is the author of two non-fiction books and many magazine and newspaper articles. In addition to his extensive international magazine publishing experience in Europe and Asia, he also has an expansive background in product development and overall magazine business administration. He has had primary responsibility in many successful magazine launches, a video production company and an internet provider company, and has developed editorial and sales and marketing programs for many multi-media projects. Moreover, he has a proven track record of converting profit-losing magazine publishing operations into profit gainers.

Monti holds a publishing diploma from New York University, and is a popular speaker at many magazine conferences including The Folio:Shows, The Circulation Management Expo & Conference, The Magazine Publishers Association Professional Development Program, and regional magazine association conferences.

ALSO BY RALPH MONTI

I Remember Brooklyn:
   Memories of Famous Sons and Daughters

Bet On Your Golf Game!
   An Indispensable Guide for Betting on the Golf Course

ACKNOWLEDGMENTS

There are several people who graciously offered their expert advice in shaping the various chapters of this book. I wish to thank Gene Sittenfeld of Gene Sittenfeld Direct Marketing, John Morthanos of Primedia, Irwin Billman of Magazine Communications Consultants, Michael Enright of Macmillan Digital USA, Joe Bertolino of the Hearst Distribution Group, Glenn Fillipone of American Lawyer Media and Ernie Parada of Cherry Lane Publishing LLC. Thanks also to Norma Jean DeVico of Carpe Diem Communications. And to Jeff Bauer, who edited the manuscript.

And finally a special, loving thank you to my wife Margaret, who conceived the idea of this book and set me on my way.

DEDICATION

To John-Carlo

May all the wonders that you envision
bring you dreams realized and hopes fulfilled.

C

TABLE OF CONTENTS

I

INTRODUCTION: WHY MAGAZINE PUBLISHING AS A CAREER?

It was a hot, sunny day in August. It was the Friday before Labor Day Weekend. While America was getting ready to celebrate its end-of-the summer holiday, I was sitting in a stuffy waiting room in Amsterdam, Holland. My heart was pounding with excitement as I paced back and forth. My baby was being born, and I was nervous as hell.

My baby was a 74-page magazine. It was being born in all its beautiful four-color glory as I waited adjacent to my printer's press room. I had been waiting for what seemed like an eternity for this moment, and the anticipation of seeing it, touching it and smelling it was killing me.

Just a year before I had come up with a nutty idea of publishing a magazine in Europe that would be distributed at trade fairs across the European continent. I had pitched the idea to my boss, who thought I was nuts and looked at me as if I had two more heads next to the inflated one that already existed. This was before the era of globalization, web sites and even fax machines. The idea of publishing a magazine in Holland, when you're a twenty-something editor in the United States with only four years in the business, was as farfetched an idea to him as publishing on the moon.

I had pitched it to my colleagues, too, who thought it an interesting idea, but not worth the risk. Somehow, though, I couldn't get the idea

My baby was a 74-page magazine.

I decided to go for it on my own.

out of my head. After several weeks of late-night thinking, I decided to go for it on my own. The problem was money. Or better said, the lack thereof. I turned to my father and pitched the idea to him. Without a second of hesitation, he wrote out a check. To this day, I often wonder what he was really thinking. I have a feeling he was just as skeptical as everyone else, but he decided to give me and my crazy dream a shot anyway. That's what made him such a terrific businessman. He wasn't afraid of a challenge or an idea, no matter how unconventional it might have seemed. And I guess he was willing to take a risk on his son.

Over the next 12 months I worked my tail off. I spent hours researching high-quality European printers who wouldn't take me to the cleaners. I worked nights calculating print bids in Italian Lira, German Mark and Dutch Guilders. I'd wake up in the middle of the night to pitch advertising to companies six hours ahead, 3,000 miles away and in languages far removed from American English. I sacrificed weekends writing the editorial, getting it translated and then proofing copy in four different languages. I negotiated barter agreements with trade fairs in return for advertising space and searched for international remailers for distribution.

The launch date was less than 12 months away, scheduled to coincide with a trade show in Cologne, Germany. I was working around the clock, seven days a week (I still kept my day job!). I remember meeting with a freelance art director in a packed bar on New Year's Eve. While everyone else was partying up a storm, I was in a corner booth with a guy named Joe fine-tuning editorial designs. And most of all, I remembering loving every minute of it!

When the door swung open and the printer came in with a dozen, "hot-off-the-press" copies of my magazine in his hand, it was a great moment. I was so ecstatic I wanted to break down in tears of joy. He made the moment more special by celebrating the birth of my new magazine with a couple of Heinekens he produced from his jacket pockets. We popped the caps, toasted my new baby and slapped each other on the back. The magazine was an instant success from year one. I paid off all my creditors, including my father, and recognized a profit to boot. The magazine went on to have a good life.

More than 15 years later, I still get excited when a magazine I publish lands on my desk. I can't tell you the number of issues I have under my belt, but each new edition still gets the juices flowing. And I've worked with lots of publishing professionals who share these same feelings. Magazine publishing is that way. It gets into your blood and it infects your soul. The intellectual energy and emotional excitement that comes from creating a magazine is very special. With more than 20 years in publishing, I'm just as charged about coming to the office today as I was my first day. There are the constant challenges to be met. New magazine ideas to be discussed. Exciting spin-offs to promote. Electronic publishing formats to be explored. There's something profoundly exciting about tapping into your creative and competitive psyche as you publish against other smart publishers.

Magazine publishing gets into your blood and it infects your soul.

19

If you embark upon a publishing career, you won't be bored or disappointed.

If you embark upon a publishing career, I guarantee you won't be bored or disappointed. This career guide was inspired by my interviewing hundreds of applicants for all different positions in the magazine publishing business. Many came to the interview with no idea about how magazine publishing works. All they brought with them were their innate talents and enthusiasm. And over the years I saw many of these smart, motivated employees grow to great successes. Native intelligence and enthusiasm are fine for the short-term. But if you really want to succeed and grow professionally in this business, it's important that you grasp the big picture of magazine publishing.

By reading this book you'll get a detailed analysis of the three central disciplines of magazine publishing—editorial, circulation and advertising—and learn what career opportunities each discipline offers. In the same way, you'll also learn about the support systems in the magazine publishing business such as production, promotion and accounting.

You'll also learn who the major companies are in the magazine business. What are the associations, trade shows and industry magazines that are part of the magazine business? What are the trends of the magazine industry? Why magazine companies are diversifying into electronic publishing—and how those avenues of publishing have opened greater career opportunities. What colleges offer the best undergraduate, post-graduate, and extension magazine publishing programs? What is your salary potential in this business? There's also a chapter on the legal land mines inherent in the magazine publishing business. And there are chapters on personnel agencies active in magazine publishing, practical information on landing a job in magazine publishing and a glossary of magazine terms. And for the aspiring magazine entrepreneur, I've included a magazine operating statement.

Francis Bacon put it best when he said, "Knowledge is power." The more you know about this business, the faster you'll succeed. And with success comes more money. But my personal philosophy is to commit your heart and soul to your work first. If you focus on doing great work, success and money will surely follow. Keep this axiom in your back pocket. It makes the journey more enjoyable.

Ralph Monti

Learn as much as possible about magazine publishing.

Author's note: A note on the choice of pronouns concerning the use of the masculine form when exploring career opportunities: I am aware some readers may be offended, but after careful analysis, the options of repeatedly using he or she or alternating the use of the masculine and feminine form did not demonstrate the ease and clarity of text when used with a consistent form. I therefore chose the masculine form.

And finally, this: The book is designed to provide information in regard to the subject matter covered. It is sold with the understanding that the publisher and the author are not engaged in rendering legal or other professional services. If legal or other expert assistance is required, the services of a competent professional should be sought.

21

If you focus on doing great work, success and money will surely follow.

It is not the purpose of this book to reprint all the information that is otherwise available to the author and/or publisher, but to complement, amplify and supplement other texts. You are urged to read all the available material, learn as much as possible about magazine publishing and to apply the information to your individual career goals.

Every effort has been made to make the book as complete and as accurate as possible. However, there may be mistakes both typographical and in content. Therefore, this text should be used only as a general guide and not looked upon to guarantee professional success. Furthermore, this book contains information and data on the magazine publishing business only up to the printing date.

The purpose of this book is to educate and entertain. The author and Special Interest Media shall have neither liability nor responsibility to any person or entity with respect to any loss or damage caused, or alleged to be caused, directly or indirectly by the information contained in this book.

1

THE HISTORY OF THE MAGAZINE BUSINESS

In 1741, when Benjamin Franklin began publishing America's first monthly magazine called *The General Magazine and Historical Chronicle, For All the British Plantations in America,* he started an American industry that would endure and flourish for centuries. For the past 250 years, magazines have disseminated information and opinion. They have reported, commented, advised and entertained. They have affected social, political and economic thought. They have been national educators and a literary force. And as we enter the new millennium, magazines have begun to evolve into newer formats as publishers revolutionize the way editorial content is delivered.

So just what is a magazine today? Is it a colorful, glossy paper product that's a cross between a book and newspaper which we either purchase on a newsstand or receive through the mail? Or is it the hot new web site, replete with slick animated graphics and chat rooms? Or maybe it's the CD-ROM? Or the 'Zine that we can't wait to buy at our favorite bookstore? Whatever form a magazine takes, all these mediums are ongoing conversations with an editor and his staff and their readers.

If we were to apply the original definition of the word magazine to any of the above, then all could be defined as a magazine. The word magazine is derived from the French word *magasin,*

For the past 250 years, magazines have disseminated information and opinion.

A diverse and invigorating future of the magazine business lies ahead.

which means a general storehouse. The earliest magazines, first appearing in France, were really catalogs of bookseller's storehouses. As these catalogs evolved, essays and articles were added. Soon these periodicals were looked on as "storehouses of reading and knowledge." When the word was brought to America, it was applied to periodicals like Franklin's *General Magazine.* So if the edgy style of today's web sites, CD-ROMs and 'Zines are all storehouses of reading and knowledge, and they all in their own way are an editor's conversation with a reader (or user), can we justifiably apply the word magazine to them? I think so. And that's exactly what makes embarking on a career in magazine publishing today such an exciting prospect: the diverse and invigorating future of the magazine business that lies ahead, not only on the printed page, but through electronic publishing too.

Without question, the magazine business today is in the midst of the most revolutionary and innovative era of its time. With innovative desktop technology and the emergence of the internet, magazines are sprouting up faster now than at any time before. In fact, over the last few years, there has been a record number of new magazine launches. And these launches have been started up and conceived by companies as diverse as the single entrepreneur to the multimedia conglomerate.

Franklin's magazine contained wit, information and wisdom of the day. It reported on matters important to the general populace. It inspired more than a dozen other magazines in colonial America. And it was the seed that would germinate a landscape of other general interest magazines in years to come. Through the 1850s magazines like *Harper's Monthly* and *Atlantic Monthly* offered literary fare from American writers. And as the Civil War approached, magazines began taking a journalistic bent, widely reporting and offering opinions on the issues dividing the States.

By the end of the 19th century and into the first part of the 20th century, magazine titles like *National Geographic, Reader's Digest, Time* and *Life* began taking root in modern American society. And as the 20th century further evolved, more magazines were brought to the marketplace that on one hand would reflect American culture, and in other instances conflict with American mores.

Indeed, no other country in the world experienced the explosive growth of magazines that America has in the 20th century. We need to thank the writers of the Bill of Rights for blessing American society with the freedom of the press, so that we Americans can publish whatever we choose. A crucial test of the freedom of the press took place in the early '50s. When Hugh Hefner first published *Playboy Magazine* as an alternative magazine to the mainstream press of that era, there were loud and passionate calls for censorship. Justice and the Constitution nevertheless prevailed.

Yet another magazine conceived to reflect "radical" American cultural tastes of its time was *Rolling Stone*. While the music and the magazine were termed counterculture phenomena by cultural observers of the '60s, what few realized was

We Americans can publish whatever we choose.

> There were no magazines on the market satisfying his curiosity, so Wenner started his own.

that these "counterculture" marvels were slowly evolving into the fabric of mainstream America. *Rolling Stone* was started in the 1960s by a young music fan from San Francisco named Jann Wenner, who wanted to read about rock music and celebrate the cultural revolution of the times. Frustrated by the fact that there were no other magazines on the market satisfying his curiosity, Wenner started his own.

With the "me" and "greed" decades of the '70s and '80s, new magazines came to the American marketplace to reflect the culture of those decades. Aptly titled magazines like *Self* and *Money* made the scene during these decades, followed by the increased popularity of magazines like *Cosmopolitan*, whose mission was "to teach women to have it all." *Esquire*, by far the most popular male magazine during the '80s, celebrated the self-indulgent yuppie lifestyle.

Since you need to be in tiptop shape to make lots of money, America saw the fitness boom take off in the mid-'80s. So while *Money* was offering tips on portfolio diversity, fitness magazines like *Running* listed ways to lower your cholesterol. And as we progressed into the '90s and the baby boom generation began settling down and having babies out in the suburbs, magazines such as *Parents*, *Family Fun*, and *Child* came to the fore.

Today's cultural trends reflected in the magazine business include the wide range of internet magazines. Other hot categories are teen titles (for the children of the baby boomers!), 50+ titles for the aging boomer market and ethnic titles for the growing populations of the African-American, Hispanic and Asian communities.

THE HISTORY OF THE MAGAZINE BUSINESS

And today's publisher has also expanded beyond general interest titles and has zeroed in on special interest markets of a general category. Many of these magazines, first called "niche" publications, have evolved into what I like to call "microniche" publications. Let's look at the boating and yachting category. It wasn't too long ago that there were only a few general interest titles that existed in the boating and yachting category. Today there are more than 60 titles in the field, and countless web sites! Titles such as *Florida Sportsman, Boating For Women, Cruising World, Chesapeake Bay Magazine, Jet Sports, Hot Boats* and *Marlin* are just a few examples.

Niche or special interest publishing can be found in virtually every category in the magazine business. Supplementing the general interest magazines that continue to remain healthy despite this trend towards niche publishing, special interest publishers are launching magazines to meet every conceivable interest. *Gun Dog* is edited for outdoorsman who own upland bird or waterfowl dogs. *Muscle Mustangs and Fast Fords* is written for automotive enthusiasts who own late-model Mustangs and Fords. *Kitchen Garden* is a food gardening magazine for home gardeners who like to cook. *Vietnam Magazine* is devoted to the Vietnam conflict and edited for both veterans of the war and students of military history.

Trade or business-to-business magazines, which represent a huge and lucrative segment of the magazine publishing business, play an equally important role. Trade magazine publishing is inherently special interest publishing. Magazines

Special interest publishers are launching magazines to meet every conceivable interest.

Four out of five households subscribe to at least one magazine.

on the trade side range from publications written for caretakers of cemeteries and sporting goods retailers to interior designers and waste management engineers.

With more than 10,000 magazines published in North America, you realize how healthy and progressive the magazine business is today. According to the Magazine Publishers of America, it is an industry that bills $10 billion in advertising revenue. Four out of five households subscribe to at least one magazine. Each household purchases an average of six different magazine titles a year off the newsstand. Indeed, 87% of the entire U.S. population, 18 years or older, reads one or more magazine during the average month. There are close to 2,000 on-line magazines today, with new additions increasing daily. It is an exciting industry that continues to evolve, and will most certainly thrive in the 21st century. So it's a great time to join in on the fun.

2

THE BASICS OF MAGAZINE PUBLISHING

To the uninitiated, magazine publishing looks like a difficult and very complex business. In many ways it is just that. It is a very intense, competitive business where you are judged on the last issue you produce. Publish a few stinkers in a row, and your readers and advertisers will run for the hills and find your competition.

While successfully publishing a magazine is no easy task, understanding the elements that make up magazine publishing is not rocket science, either. The best way I've explained the intricacies of publishing to my students and prospective employees new to publishing is with an analogy I was taught early in my career. It goes like this: Think of magazine publishing as a three-legged stool. The first leg is editorial. The second is circulation. And the third, final leg is advertising. Put them all together equally and you have a well-balanced magazine. Once you understand that all three are related and should be treated equally, you will have a basic understanding of why some magazines succeed and others fail. When building the successful "magazine stool," the leg that goes on first is editorial, followed by circulation (readership) and then advertising. But before we take a look at each of these elements, let's take a look at the state of the job market in magazine publishing today.

In the magazine publishing business you are judged on the last issue you publish.

Growth in magazine positions has increased four to five percent.

THE JOB LANDSCAPE TODAY

Over the last decade, the job market in magazine publishing has changed dramatically. Like many other industries, magazine publishing has seen its share of downsizing, retrenchment, mergers and many, many acquisitions. There has been a "flattening" of the magazine publishing organizational charts, resulting in the disappearance of many middle-management positions. All this sound familiar? Despite these trends, growth in magazine positions over the same period has increased four to five percent. Not great growth, but not bad, either. Despite these modest figures, the number of magazines on the market has increased precipitously.

Industry trend monitors have shown steady growth in special interest and business-to-business magazines. A large part of that growth has been the many introductions of computer titles that have kept pace with the dramatic growth of the computer business itself. This being said, even when we discount the computer titles, the industry still has shown steady growth and remains healthy.

Through the '90s, some trends that have evolved include the globalization of the magazine industry—more foreign companies are publishing in the United States or own a substantial share in heretofore privately owned American companies. There has also been a substantial increase of capital into the magazine business from Wall Street. So how does this affect you, the prospective magazine employee? From these forces, many magazine jobs have either changed completely, have evolved into positions defined by a whole new set of parameters, or have been slightly redefined. Let's look at editorial positions as an example. Many writers and editors are working from their homes these days. With the advancement of today's communications technology, it is not unheard of for the editor of a consumer magazine (those magazines you subscribe to or purchase off a newsstand) or business-to-business magazine (those magazines written for readers working in a specific industry) to oversee the magazine from his home, many miles from the main office. Indeed, many magazines count on writers, copy editors, reporters, etc., for stories generated on the home computer. This was not the case years before.

Advanced computer technology has redefined the role of the production staff (the folks in charge of actually manufacturing the magazine). It's extremely critical that today's production staff be up-to-date on the latest print and prepress technology. Digitized advertising is being sent to production departments from advertising agencies bent on pushing the technology envelope. Magazine printing technology is becoming more advanced and complex, and paper costs (usually the biggest cost in the manufacturing of a magazine) have been volatile over the last several years due to global forces. The keen production staff stays on top of all these trends by increased trips to the company's printer, attending industry seminars on the latest production technology and voraciously reading articles in the industry trade magazines.

Yet another job revolution has developed in the circulation department (the folks in charge of

Printing technology is becoming more advanced and complex.

Today's circulation professionals are known as consumer marketing directors.

finding readers). Today's circulation professionals arc being relied on to grow a magazine's business through the emergence of brand extensions—spin-offs from the core magazine franchise. This was not the case years before. Circulators in the past were looked at strictly as reader bean counters, while the advertising sales staff owned the mandate of growing the magazine's business. Indeed, even the titles have changed in the circulation department. Many of today's circulation professionals are now known as consumer marketing directors, a role that demands financial and database skills as well as product creativity. The expansion of responsibilities in this department has led to more circulation people gaining access to senior management, traditionally a path reserved for the advertising sales staff. In fact, the greatest demand for talent in the magazine business today lies in finding solid circulation professionals. Indeed, a good circulation professional today can command a high compensation package.

While circulation professionals have emerged as important revenue generators, advertising sales executives still play a major role in the magazine industry. How they go about their business today is again light years away from how they conducted business just 10 years ago. Advertising sales presentations have become more sophisticated today, with many ad sales executives now using CD-ROM presentations, videos, teleconferencing and e-mail as a way to sell and educate their customers. While all of this will never replace the age-old face-to-face meeting, today's advanced technology has made the ad sales executive more immediately responsive to his client.

With the advent of more titles on the market, competition for a finite universe of advertising sales dollars has forced the smarter advertising staff to become more creative. Today's advertising sales presentation will usually include a "value-added" program that will offer a variety of programs to the prospective client beyond the advertising space buy. These programs can include event marketing for the client, sponsorship opportunities for future editorial supplements, or a subscription sweepstakes partnership with the magazine. So yet another evolution in the ad sales department has been the demand for ad sales executives to be more creative in their sales approach through the creation of these value-added programs.

Now that we have analyzed the state of the magazine industry, let's examine how the central disciplines of publishing—editorial, circulation and advertising—combine to make a magazine.

Competition has forced the advertising staff to become more creative.

THE EDITORIAL DEPARTMENT

If the magazine doesn't serve an editorial mission or purpose, it will have a very short life. Just like people, all magazines are born, have a life and, at some point, die.

Some magazines die early. Others stumble along during their life, and some stay on life support for too many years. Others enjoy a happy, healthy life that can go on for decades.

So why do some magazines die early while others thrive? There are a variety of reasons, not the least of which is undercapitalization. But let's

A magazine's editorial mission must be based on solid ground.

concentrate on the editorial aspect of why magazines fail in today's marketplace.

Most importantly, a magazine's editorial mission must be based on solid ground. Trends in society will generally dictate the launch of new magazines, but it is the astute and successful publisher who understands the difference between a trend and a fad. If a magazine is launched from a societal fad, once the fad disappears, the magazine will die as well. Magazines based on fads don't have a long life. But basic trends and societal mores can breathe life into a magazine for many, many years.

Let's take a look at some of the strongest and longest-running magazine franchises on the market today—*Time*, *People*, *GQ*, *Good Housekeeping* and *Vogue*. You'll notice a strong and finely-honed editorial mission within each of these magazines. They all understand what their editorial mission is, and they know exactly how to go about fulfilling that mission with great aplomb. Each serves broad interests that lie within the fabric of American society: news, celebrity and style. News will certainly never go out of fashion. The allure of celebrity—the editorial mission of *People*—will always be "in." Men's and women's fashion magazines have always been strong, as has women's service magazines like *Good Housekeeping*.

So why do these magazines succeed while competitive titles fail? The secret to the success of these magazines is that they are addressing a long-term reader need and they are being guided by an editor with a strong vision. This vision is the magazine's editorial direction, which continuously evolves, but it does so with careful subtlety so that most times the readers don't even recognize change is taking place. If you were to compare today's issues of these magazines with an issue that was published just five years ago, you would notice these changes.

How does a magazine evolve editorially without readers even noticing? Like people, magazines have personalities that must develop and grow over time. While the overall personality of the magazine might stay the same, the nuances and underlying colorations that make up the personality change constantly. With a magazine, it can be a slight slant on how features or articles are written. It can be the addition or deletion of a column. A subtle change in type style can make a magazine page look more "newsy" or more feature-like. The use of photos can change over the course of time. All of these elements give the magazine its look and feel.

An editor uses these elements to fashion the direction of a magazine, much like a sculptor uses clay to craft a piece of sculpture. We'll get into more of this in greater depth later on. The point is, when a magazine is being shaped by a great editor, the greater the editor's skills, the less readers notice. What they do notice is that they like the magazine, it feels and reads good to them, and they want to buy and read every issue.

Now let's take a look at why magazines fail editorially. Sometimes over the course of its life, a magazine loses its direction because its editor has lost his direction. Or the magazine loses steam because it hasn't stayed up with the times. Editors are human. Personal or professional

Like people, magazines have personalities that must develop and grow over time.

39

Most strong editors are benevolent dictators with a vision.

problems can interfere with their vision. Or they just get burned out after guiding a magazine over a period of years. Sometimes, other forces are at play, such as a meddling owner or publisher interfering with the editor. All of these factors spell doom. Without a clearly-focused editorial direction set by the editor, a magazine will rapidly fall out of sync with its readers. And once that happens the magazine will begin to deteriorate.

This is not to suggest that editors are God. The more successful editors will tell you that while they have final say over what goes into their magazines, they seek out and weigh very carefully what their associates and readers have to say. They evaluate, distill and analyze all ideas, and use or not use them accordingly. Most strong editors are benevolent dictators with a vision. In many ways, editors are like movie directors or symphony conductors. They rely on the genius of their contemporaries but it's their genius to set the broad parameters. It has always been my contention that success in magazine publishing starts with having a talented and enthusiastic editor. A great magazine product conceived and implemented by the editor will attract readers, which in turn will generate advertising revenue.

CIRCULATION

You can have a magazine with compelling editorial and inspiring photography, but if no one reads it, you'll be out of business in no time. Circulation directors or consumer marketing directors are the people responsible for finding and renewing readers for magazines. Finding

THE BASICS OF MAGAZINE PUBLISHING

and renewing readers is an expensive, time-consuming process, but one that is paramount to the health of a magazine. Remember, readers are the second leg for the successful magazine stool, so without readers, advertisers won't advertise.

For consumer magazine circulation directors, finding readers is done through a variety of sources, but essentially it is achieved through two sources: direct mail marketing and newsstand sales. Volumes have been written about the science and art of direct mail subscription marketing, but the bottom line is it works (although not as well as in years past). And it has gotten very expensive for magazine publishers over the years. There are other avenues to generate readership, but for the most part the majority of magazine publishers use direct mail. Larger publishing companies will supplement their direct mail efforts through ongoing telemarketing campaigns, television and a variety of other alternate sources of subscription promotion their circulation directors can cultivate.

Finding readers is done through a variety of sources.

While the process of finding new readers is going on, renewing present readers must take place. Renewals are as important to the health of a magazine as finding new readers. This is accomplished through a constant mailing of renewal series or renewal efforts. Depending on a magazine's budget and size, a renewal series can consist of six to nine pieces of mail. Astute circulation directors realize they are most likely dealing with three kinds of subscribers: those passionate readers who will walk to a publisher's offices to buy the magazine; those who feel they can live without their publication; and the enor-

41

Newsstand distribution has changed dramatically.

mous group in between who need to be sold and renewed. This is the group that is important to the profitability of the magazine. Affecting the new subscriber or renewal rate is the offer. The offer is the price and term (how long) of the subscription. Many mailings are done to test offers. This is where the art and science of subscription marketing comes into play.

The process of finding readers for business magazines has its own peculiarities. Generally, mailing lists can be purchased specific to the industry to which a new trade magazine is geared. The magazine is mailed to the individuals on the list and then a qualification process begins. This qualification process is mandated by the United States Post Office and private auditing companies. Essentially, it monitors and prevents the unscrupulous practice of falsifying readership numbers. Reader qualification must be done every year, and it's an expensive, time-consuming process. Readership numbers are important because they affect advertising rates.

A large percentage (and in some cases the only source) of many consumer magazines' readership comes from the newsstand. Over the last several years, newsstand distribution of the magazine business has changed dramatically—and not to the benefit of the magazine publisher. Today's best-selling newsstand outlets are in supermarkets, airports, bookstores, convenience store chains, drug store chains and mass merchandisers.

These retailers are demanding and getting better terms from the wholesalers who supply them with their magazines. The wholesalers in turn are passing these costs on to the magazine publisher. These new terms have squeezed publisher profits. But while these changes of fortune have caused newsstand distribution to be in a state of flux, the newsstand remains a vital distribution source for the consumer magazine company.

ADVERTISING

Once a magazine rounds up a significant number of readers through direct mail or newsstand, and the second leg is securely fastened to the successful magazine stool, it's time for the third and final leg—selling advertising in the magazine. Advertising plays an extremely prominent role in the magazine business. It is a very important revenue stream, and for many trade or business-to-business magazines, it is the only revenue stream. Indeed, when a publisher considers launching a magazine, one of the initial elements he assesses is the magazine's advertising potential.

For a consumer magazine, the publisher evaluates its advertising potential on two levels. First, he takes a look at the endemic advertising universe—advertisers whose corporate mission parallels the editorial direction of the magazine. Once that universe has been established, he carefully evaluates the universe of non-endemic advertisers, companies peripheral to the field and complementary to the readers.

Here's an example. Suppose a general interest automotive magazine is being evaluated for a launch. The publisher looks at the endemic universe and concludes that automobile manufacturers—like Ford, General Motors, Nissan and Toyota—and tire companies—like Goodyear,

When a publisher considers launching a magazine, he assesses the magazine's advertising potential.

43

Magazine print advertising is just one part of the marketing mix.

Michelin, and BFGoodrich—are the target endemic advertisers. The non-endemic universe would include hotels and resorts, cigarettes, fashion and liquor accounts—companies that the readers of automotive magazines will also have an interest in. On the business magazine side, advertising generally represents the magazine's only revenue stream. We'll explore business magazines in greater detail in a later chapter, but for the most part these magazines generate most of their revenues from advertising. There is very little, if any, revenue generated from the reader side in terms of subscriptions or newsstand sales. Most business magazines are mailed free to interested readers.

Because of the nature of their editorial mission, trade magazines carry advertising endemic to the industry they serve. It is unusual to see non-endemic company advertising in such a magazine. So if a business magazine covers the office supply industry, you will see lots of advertising for office supplies. It is highly unlikely that you will see advertising for any other product or service beyond that.

Companies that usually advertise in magazines most often are promoting their product or service through other avenues, too. Magazine print advertising is just one part of their marketing mix. Depending on the size of the company, print advertising is supplemented with advertising on television, radio, the web, direct mail, billboards, event marketing and other media. Competition is fierce among advertising salespeople to persuade companies to advertise in their magazines. In today's marketplace, there are very few magazines that publish without competition.

THE SUCCESSFUL EQUATION
When you have all three elements (editorial, advertising and circulation) working together, you most likely will have a profitable magazine. Coordinating the editorial strategy with the efforts of the advertising and circulation departments is the publisher's job. The publisher must create an environment that assures all three elements are working harmoniously. The publisher must keep in mind that the company's "product" is the content and design of the magazine's editorial mission. As I stated previously, the whole process starts with the editor. Too often, because of their lack of experience, or because most publishers rise to upper management through the advertising sales side, some publishers simply don't recognize this maxim. They try to sell their magazine to readers or advertisers based on short-term deals or strategies.

At a recent publishing conference where I was a seminar speaker, I was sitting with an editor who was overseeing a very well-known, very profitable magazine for Time Inc. When I asked her about how she works with her publisher and business colleagues, she mentioned that the business staff of her magazine was an extremely smart bunch with a great editorial vision. "They are as smart as the editorial staff," she quipped sarcastically. I knew what she was hinting at. Too often the business side of a magazine company works counter to its editorial staff. Many salespeople unjustifiably view the editorial text as the stuff that fills the pages between advertising. For

> **A publishing company's "product" is the content and design of the magazine's editorial mission.**

45

Learn the culture of the companies you interview with.

this reason, its not uncommon for the editorial people on a magazine to work adversely with the advertising people, and vice-versa. This is an unfortunate commentary on the magazine business—and for the most part we're talking about companies less smart and less successful than Time Inc.

As you begin your search to land a position in magazine publishing, strive to learn the culture of the companies you interview with. Is it a company that values editorial visions to sell advertising? Are they sincerely interested in fulfilling their readers' needs? Do the editors, circulation people and advertising people all share in the equity of the company's success? If the answer to all three questions is yes, you've found yourself a good magazine publishing company. Make haste to sign on.

3

CONSUMER VS. BUSINESS-TO-BUSINESS PUBLISHING

Many people have heard of Tina Brown, the much-publicized former editor of *The New Yorker*. When Tina left *The New Yorker* to go Hollywood, reams of articles were written in newspapers and newsweeklies across the country. Her departure was even reported on the front page (over the fold!) of *The New York Times*. But few people know who is the editor of *Progressive Grocer*.

As it happens, *Progressive Grocer* is a business-to-business magazine that reports on the supermarket and grocery business. What's important to understand is that *Progressive Grocer* goes about its business basically the same way as *The New Yorker* (with obviously less glitz). It is a well-respected magazine whose editor is well-known and highly influential in the supermarket industry. As you might recall, business-to-business (or trade) magazines serve a specific industrial, business, service or professional audience. You won't find most of these magazines on newsstands. Most are mailed free to people working in the industry they report on. Like consumer magazines, successful trade magazines are run by dedicated and intelligent publishing people. The difference is business-to-business magazine publishing is not as glamorous to the layperson.

So if you're dazzled by the glamour aspect as you plan your magazine publishing career, then certainly the consumer side of the magazine

Progressive Grocer **goes about its business basically the same way as** *The New Yorker.*

Trade publications play a vital role in the industries they write about.

business is for you. Most people have heard of *Esquire* or *Newsweek*. But very few have heard about *Casual Living*, *Auto Laundry News*, *Meetings & Conventions* or *Toy and Hobby World*. Unless you are in the casual furniture business, the carwash industry, the convention planning business or the toy industry, you will have no interest in these magazines. Yet these publications play a vital role in the industries they write about. They keep their readers informed on industry issues and up-to-date on trends and news.

Outside of the glamour aspect, working in trade magazine publishing is generally the same as consumer magazine publishing. The only difference is pay scale. But unlike what most people would guess, trade magazine publishing generally pays better. I've published on both sides, and each has its advantages and disadvantages. It all comes down to the magazine and/or company you're with. There are extremely interesting, fun-filled, and dynamic magazines (and companies) in both areas. There are also dull, lackluster and boring publications on both sides, too. If you want to break into the publishing business, chances are you're not going to have much say in your break-in magazine assignment. Nevertheless, I've always felt your job is what you make it. And if you fall head over heels with the publishing process in general, writing about successful trends in the supermarket industry for *Progressive Grocer* can be just as exciting and interesting as writing about the top 10 fashion tips for men in *Esquire*.

Or selling advertising to upscale furniture

manufacturers can be as challenging and reward-ing as selling to General Motors. If you disagree, then look for a job on the consumer side of pub-lishing.

There are hundreds of publishers in today's marketplace, publishing thousands of magazine titles. Many publishers are small one- or two-per-son operations. Some are media conglomerates. The majority of magazine publishers fall some-where in between, with employee numbers at all levels. As you begin your search for an opportu-nity in magazine publishing, it's good to know who the top players are. Here's a sampling of some of the larger magazine companies.

CONSUMER MAGAZINE COMPANIES

Condé Nast Publications
There is probably no consumer publisher in the magazine business more glamorous than Condé Nast Publications. If you're looking for a com-pany whose editors reputedly proof copy in Armani or Donna Karan suits, Condé is for you. They are recognized as a magazine pub-lisher that produces highly stylized, excellent editorial and—the Armani suits notwithstand-ing—aggressive, street-smart tactics on the advertising and circulation side. Their publica-tions include *GQ, Condé Nast Traveler, Vogue, Architectural Digest, Gourmet* and *Mademoiselle.*
Condé Nast Publications Inc.
350 Madison Avenue
New York, NY 10017
Tel: (212)-880-8800

There are hundreds of publishers in today's marketplace.

Hearst is a solid magazine company whose revenues remain strong.

Hearst Corporation
Hearst is the home of *Esquire, Good House-keeping, Cosmopolitan, Redbook, Harper's Bazaar* and many other fine publications. They have gone through some management changes over the years, but the company's revenues remain strong, and their magazines continue to grow. Hearst is a solid organization that has divisions addressing a variety of magazine disciplines. They represent other magazine publishers for newsstand distribution and other services.
Hearst Corporation
959 Eighth Avenue
New York, New York 10019
Tel: (212)-649-2000

PRIMEDIA
PRIMEDIA is a highly diverse magazine publisher that has in their stable venerable magazines like *New York, Automobile, Modern Bride, Seventeen* and many, many others on both the consumer and business sides. They have grown through an aggressive acquisition strategy. Although viewed by some in the magazine business as an investment banking company disguised as a magazine publisher, PRIMEDIA continues to grow as it continues to acquire.
PRIMEDIA
717 Fifth Avenue
New York, NY 10151
Tel: (212)-745-0500

Rodale Press, Inc.
Rodale Press is a first-class magazine publisher that publishes many health and fitness maga-

zines, like *Prevention, Bicycling, Scuba Diving, Backpacker* and *Runner's World.* Their mid-'90s launch, *Men's Health,* has evolved into a very hot property. Its success led other publishing companies to jump into the men's fitness and health category.

Rodale Press Inc.
33 E. Minor Street
Emmaus, PA 18098
Tel: (610) 967-5171
Fax: (610) 967-8963

Time Inc.
The publisher of *Time, Money, Life, People, Sports Illustrated* and *Fortune* just keeps getting better and better as it gets bigger and bigger. They have spun off other titles over the last several years, and also have a custom publishing program. Despite their corporate behemoth size, they have a reputation—earned over the last several years—of letting their people work and flourish independently.

Time-Life Building
1271 Avenue of the Americas
New York, NY 10020
Tel: (212) 522-1212

BUSINESS-TO-BUSINESS MAGAZINE COMPANIES

BPI Communications Inc.
BPI publishes a slew of magazines, many for the music and entertainment businesses. With titles like *The Hollywood Reporter, Back Stage* and *Amusement Business,* how can you not have

How can you not have fun working at BPI?

fun working at BPI? BPI also has a division called *AdWeek Magazines* that reports on the advertising and media industries.
BPI Communications Inc.
1515 Broadway
New York, NY 10036
Tel: (212) 764-7300

Cahners Publishing Company,
a division of Reed Elsevier
With its huge Cahners division, Reed Elsevier is an international publisher with roots in Holland and the United Kingdom. Reed Elsevier and Cahners have a diverse empire of business-to-business magazines built mainly through acquisitions. While many of the titles are industrial in nature, it is a company that is solidly built and smartly managed.
Cahners Publishing Company,
a division of Reed Elsevier
275 Washington Street
Newton, MA 02158
Tel: (617) 964-3030

Crain Communications, Inc.
Like other magazine publishing companies, Crain is a family-owned business that dates back several generations. It is headquartered in Chicago, but has offices around the country. Crain publishes prestigious magazines like *Advertising Age*, which reports on the advertising and communications industries, and *Automotive News*, which covers the automotive business. They also publish a number of other trade magazines.

Crain Communications, Inc.
740 N. Rush
Chicago, Illinois 60611
Tel: (312) 649-5200

The McGraw-Hill Companies
McGraw-Hill is a top business-to-business magazine publisher that also publishes *BusinessWeek*, one of the top consumer business magazines. It is a very diverse communications company that also publishes textbooks and newsletters. McGraw-Hill publishes magazines for a variety of industries, including construction, aviation and chemical engineering.
The McGraw-Hill Companies
1221 Avenue of the Americas
New York, NY 10020
Tel: (212) 512-2000

Miller Freeman, Inc.
This San Francisco-based publisher has offices around the country with divisions in New York and Dallas. Miller Freeman publishes a wide selection of business-to-business magazines, with title ranging from *National Jeweler* to *Digital Video Magazine*. They are known for their solid editorial, and smart circulation and advertising marketing.
Miller Freeman, Inc.
600 Harrison Street
San Francisco, CA 94107
Tel: (415)905-2200

Miller Freeman is known for solid editorial, and smart circulation and advertising marketing.

These companies represent some of the larger publishing companies in the consumer and trade magazine businesses. This list is by no means meant to be interpreted as the "best in the business." There are many other high quality publishing companies like The Petersen Companies, Ziff-Davis Publishing, ABC, Inc., IDG Communications, Penton Publishing, Inc., Advanstar and CMP Communications. There are also small magazine publishing companies, those who employ less than 100 employees—some even less than 50 people—who are known in the magazine publishing business as publishers of distinction.

4

AN INSIDE LOOK: THE BUSINESS SIDE OF MAGAZINE PUBLISHING

Now that you have some general knowledge of magazine publishing, let's start taking an even closer look at the business.

Almost every magazine has a masthead. What's a masthead? Usually found within the first few pages of a magazine, it's a listing of people who make up the staff of that particular magazine. Larger companies also list their corporate officers and board of directors.

One of the big thrills you'll have when you land your first job in the magazine publishing business is seeing your name on a magazine's masthead. It's great to show to your friends, parents, spouse or kids. It's a nice little perk that comes with the territory. What's even more fun is watching your name rise up the masthead as you succeed in your career.

One of the big thrills in magazine publishing is seeing your name on a masthead.

Over the next several chapters, we'll take a close look at all the disciplines of magazine publishing, and describe in basic terms what all the people on the masthead do. Let's start with the business side of magazine publishing first.

THE PUBLISHER

The publisher is the person who oversees the business operation of the magazine. He's directly in charge of the magazine's health and growth. His day-to-day responsibilities may include visiting with a major advertiser, meeting with the circulation director or negotiating with

The publisher has the ultimate profit and loss responsibilities for the magazine.

the newsstand company that distributes his magazine. The publisher is the person who has the ultimate profit and loss responsibilities for the magazine. If the magazine isn't doing well, it's the publisher who will incur the wrath of the owners or shareholders.

The role of the publisher can vary from company to company. A publisher at a small magazine, for example, generally will also get involved in the day-to-day selling of advertising. In the past, most people who attained the publisher's position have come from the advertising sales side of the magazine business. This has changed over the years. Today, many publishers come from the circulation side. It's not often that an editor becomes a publisher. But in rare instances it does happen. Generally, because the publisher is a "business" position, the publisher comes from the business side.

THE ADVERTISING DIRECTOR

The advertising director is the person who's in charge of selling advertising in the magazine. The advertising director can be the sole salesperson on the magazine, or he can oversee a staff of advertising people. Reporting directly to the publisher, he is the person who's in charge of preparing the sales presentations to prospective advertisers and coordinating promotional material for the magazine.

If there is a full staff of advertising people, each salesperson's responsibility is broken down either by geographical territory or category. This means that a salesperson calls on clients in a given region in the United States, or he oversees a specific advertising category like hotel accounts, liquor accounts, automotive accounts, etc. Sometimes you'll see a listing of offices geographically situated around the country. These are usually sales offices from which a one- or two-person advertising sales staff works.

Supporting the advertising sales effort may be a team of sales support professionals, ranging from a marketing director, who's in charge of selling strategies, to a merchandise manager, who develops programs that enhance advertisers' marketing strategies. In addition to marketing and merchandising, the promotion department will be called upon to create compelling written and visual material for advertising salespeople to use in their presentations. Promotion staff may also be asked to develop themes and sales materials for exhibits and meetings, or to create advertisements for trade publications. Also, the publicity or public relations department will employ strategies to attract attention to the magazine. And not to be forgotten is the research department, whose functions are to provide reader demographics to the advertising salespeople so that they may strategically position their magazine on a sales call.

> **The circulation director is in charge of keeping the readers happy and servicing their needs.**

THE CIRCULATION DIRECTOR

The circulation director is the person responsible for finding new readers for the magazine as well as renewing present readers. He is also charged with keeping the readers happy and servicing their needs as best as possible. Like the advertising director, the circulation director (or consumer marketing manager) usually reports directly

A premium is a gift the reader receives for paying for a subscription.

to the publisher. In addition to coordinating a schedule of renewal and billing campaigns—most often done on a monthly basis—the circulation director also plans "roll-outs" or large direct mail campaigns to prospective readers.

The essence of a direct mail campaign is the "offer." The basic elements of an offer are the price and payment terms the magazine offers a potential reader. There are two types of offers: a hard offer and a soft offer. A hard offer is when the prospective reader must pay the invoice first before receiving his first issue. He can then cancel the subscription anytime during the life of the subscription.

A soft offer gives the prospective reader options. He is not obligated to send money to begin receiving the subscription, and even before he sends money, he can cancel the subscription after receiving a first "free" issue. Payment terms—like "Pay in three easy installments"—may be included in a soft offer as well.

Another tactic that a circulation director has at his disposal when soliciting new readers is premiums. A premium is a gift the reader receives for paying for a subscription. These gifts can range from telephones to posters to editorial booklets. Premiums work well because they add extra value to the subscription price and therefore boost response rate. A derivative of a premium is a freemium. A freemium is what it sounds like: It's a free premium you receive in the mail to get your attention to a subscription offer.

In addition to direct mail campaigns a circulation director implements, he also explores other ways to generate readers through other avenues.

Called alternate sources, these can be in the form of DRTV (Direct Response Television), sweepstakes, stampsheets like those published by Publishers Clearing House and American Family Publishers, package inserts, supermarket "take ones", event promotions, on-box promotions and postcard decks.

Assisting the circulation director might be a circulation promotion assistant, or a subscription and fulfillment assistant. Also working closely with the circulation director might be the newsstand director.

THE NEWSSTAND DIRECTOR

The newsstand director (or single-copy sales director) is in charge of getting the magazine out to as many efficient-selling retail locations as possible. The newsstand director's challenge is to optimize penetration of his magazine against comparative titles in the category. If the magazine is the only title in the category, he'll use a demographically similar title for comparative purposes.

In recent years the organizational structure of the newsstand distribution system has changed dramatically. These changes have made competition for newsstand rack space fierce. The key word to get your magazine into a retail chain is "authorization." If your magazine is granted authorization to be on newsstands in a retail chain like 7-Eleven or Safeway, for instance, it better sell. If it doesn't, your magazine will be taken off the racks.

The hierarchy of newsstand or single-copy sales distribution works like this: The publisher

> **The key word to get your magazine into a retail chain is "authorization."**

> **The newsstand director invests money in incentives or promotions to increase the magazine's newsstand sales.**

develops print orders or allotments with its national distributor. The national distributor works as the publisher's marketer, distribution expert and "banker" by providing advances to the publisher. These advances are based on estimated net sales of the magazine. The national distributor sets a print order based on retail authorizations, and determines how many copies should be invoiced and sent to a regional wholesaler. The regional wholesaler delivers the magazines and invoices its retail accounts. The retailers place the magazine on the newsstand, checkout or mainline rack. The best-selling newsstands generally are in supermarkets, airports, bookstores, convenience store chains, drugstore chains and mass merchandisers.

Magazines are routed through this distribution process on a "returnable basis." This means that whatever copies haven't been sold are then returned to the wholesaler, where they are counted and then shredded. The difference between the number of copies returned and the number of copies shipped is the total copies sold.

The newsstand director will sometimes invest money in a variety of incentives or promotions to increase the magazine's newsstand sales or "sellthrough." Many key retail locations require placement or slotting fees in order to obtain display or distribution (airports or supermarket check-out racks, for example). Also, because of the recent changes in traditional newsstand distribution, as well as the changes in consumer shopping habits, "alternative direct-to-retail" distribution is taking place. Here, a publisher operates a direct-to-retail program to targeted retailers. Examples of

THE BUSINESS SIDE OF MAGAZINE PUBLISHING

this are music magazines found in music stores or automotive magazines found in auto parts stores. Additionally, national distributors, wholesalers and magazine publishers have developed direct-to-retail rack programs, offering limited, targeted or niche titles to proprietary retail chain accounts. These magazines are shipped to the retailer and will include only titles that are of interest to the retailers' customer base. Examples of this are home and garden magazines to garden and home centers or healthy living magazines to vitamin and health food stores. General-interest magazines and magazines out of the category are generally not shipped to this type of account.

THE MARKETING OR PROMOTION MANAGER

Many large publishers employ a marketing or promotion manager, or both. In its most strict sense, the role of these managers is to heighten the awareness of the magazine to the general public, and to make a profit to boot!

Some ways these managers accomplish this is through event marketing, trade or consumer advertising, sponsorships and affinity groups. There are literally a host of ways a magazine can be promoted, cross-merchandised or cross-branded. Just take a look at *Martha Stewart's Living Magazine*. The magazine has successfully cross-promoted and cross-merchandised its brand name on all types of consumer goods, including paint! All it takes is first having a strong magazine brand, then lots of creativity and ingenuity.

Promotion managers heighten the awareness of the magazine to the general public.

Job titles are influenced by the size and philosophy of the publishing company.

THE BUSINESS MANAGER

The business manager is the controller or financial person of the magazine. Working closely with the publisher, he handles the day-to-day accounting of the magazine company. His duties can be as narrow as analyzing the affairs of just one magazine, or as broad as handling a multititle operation that also includes the administrative financials of the company. The business manager proposes budgets, devises projection models and handles receivables that come in from advertising sales, single-copy sales, subscription sales and any ancillary revenue. Additional business personnel may also include a credit manager, an accountant, a financial analyst, and a collection person.

What's meaningful to remember is that a company's job titles are influenced by the size and philosophy of the publishing company. A person functioning as a publisher at a large magazine company like Time Inc., for example, will no doubt have responsibilities much different from a publisher working at a much smaller company. Differences in tasks and responsibilities will vary with other positions as well.

5

AN INSIDE LOOK: THE CREATIVE SIDE OF MAGAZINE PUBLISHING

In this chapter we take a look at the creative side of magazine publishing. We'll start with the editor.

THE EDITOR (OR EDITOR-IN-CHIEF)

Without question, the most critical person on the magazine staff is the editor. He is the person who sets the vision, pace, tone, style, feel and look of the magazine. The editor brings life and energy to a magazine. His mandate is to create a magazine that's inspirational, entertaining and educational. He should surprise his readers with editorial that is always fresh and cutting edge, and occasionally provocative. A good editor knows how to infuse his magazine with all these elements—and more!

There's an axiom in publishing that editors are overworked and underpaid. And except for a handful of celebrity editors in the magazine business, there is some truth to this theory. Yet I've met very few editors who dislike what they do, regardless of how overworked and underpaid they are. Editing a magazine is a wonderfully challenging job that keeps even the brightest minds on their toes.

So what does a magazine editor actually do? In addition to creating the long-term vision of the magazine, the day-to-day duties of an editor include creating and trafficking the editorial package of each issue. The editor is in charge of

The editor brings life and energy to a magazine.

Many editors do very little writing.

generating feature story ideas, assigning stories to staff and contributing (or freelance) writers, working with photographers for each article, and working with the art director on the layouts. The editor does all this under strict printing deadlines that never bend.

The editor will also be called upon to occasionally meet with advertisers over breakfast, lunch or dinner. Often, industry functions or events sponsored by advertisers necessitate his presence. The editor also fields telephone inquiries from readers, and meets with production and senior management personnel. He juggles problems that remain on one edition that must go out the door, while gearing up for the next. Editing a magazine is not for the feint of heart or squeamish. It's a tough job that demands long hours and a fast pace.

It is for these reasons that some editors are occasionally cranky, abrupt and downright rude. They keep conversations short and run through hallways at a sometimes maniacal pace. Despite this, most editors are wonderfully creative people who have extremely fertile minds and would love to sit and chat—if they had the time. But they have an issue to get out, so they'll catch you later.

Few editors grow up wanting to be an editor, though most grow up wanting to write. And therein lies the rub. Many editors do very little writing, other than their column on the editorial page. So contrary to popular thought, editors edit and writers write. Toward that end, an editor's job might be to tweak manuscripts, advise writers to rework a story or slant an article with a different voice. The editor acts as an overseer in the writing process. Indeed, the editor's job is to analyze and assess each story to determine how (and if) it fits with the other stories in the issue. He must look at each issue as a collective body of work, and work vigorously to ensure that each story nicely fits into that body. To do that he works with a variety of writers and associate editors to fine-tune the issue to his vision.

THE MANAGING EDITOR

Working closely with the editor is the managing editor. The managing editor is the person who keeps the magazine running on time. He's in charge of keeping the editorial matter flowing internally according to the deadlines posted for each issue. He works closely with the editor to obtain feature material from staff and freelance writers, and then assigns each story to a copy editor for proofing. He also traffics all the editorial into the art department for layout.

Essentially, the managing editor is the taskmaster of the editorial department. The managing editor keeps the entire editorial staff on its toes—including the editor. Too often, editors develop an aversion for deadlines. So it becomes the managing editor's responsibility to keep the editor focused on all his deadlines.

A managing editor often doubles as copy editor. A managing editor also coordinates the magazine as it is being trafficked through the advertising, production and art departments. In fact, ask a half dozen managing editors what their responsibilities are, and there's a good chance you'll get a half dozen different answers. The

The managing editor is the person who keeps the magazine running on time.

most common responsibility for a managing editor, however, is to be the person who makes sure the editorial flows easily through the publishing company.

THE COPY EDITOR

On some magazine mastheads—but certainly not all—you will see the title of "copy editor." So just what is a copy editor? A copy editor is the person responsible for proofreading every editorial piece for grammar, punctuation and style. Believe it or not, many writers—even the really good ones—don't know a dangling participle from a split infinitive (remember those from grammar school English class?). Moreover, many writers have problems spelling, or don't know whether to use a comma or a semicolon. The copy editor makes these corrections on each manuscript much like your English teacher corrected your fifth-grade essay. He formats each manuscript into proper English.

> The copy editor makes corrections on manuscripts much like your English teacher corrected your fifth-grade essay.

Beyond grammatical modifications, the copy editor also monitors each manuscript for "house style." House style refers to the consistent grammatical style favored by the publishing house, or the treatment of jargon or terms specific to the subject matter that might not be found in standard reference books. Because many English grammar rules have more than one interpretation, the copy editor makes sure that each manuscript carries the same interpretation for each article. When a copy editor first joins a magazine publishing company, he is given a style sheet that advises him of the house style.

Here's an example: Some magazine publishers

will treat the use of serial commas differently. A sentence such as "He brought his snorkel, mask and fins to the lake" can be interpreted two ways. In the above example, there is no comma after the word mask. Another house style might call for adding a comma after the word mask.

ASSOCIATE EDITORS AND CONTRIBUTING EDITORS

An associate or assistant editor is usually a staff editorial person who works with or assists the editor. His responsibilities can include writing or editing full-length feature articles as well as writing or editing photo captions, department material, product reviews or news.

A contributing editor is usually a writer who is not on staff and who writes for the magazine on a freelance or per article basis. Generally, a contributing editor has a certain expertise that is relevant to a particular interest—celebrity interviews, for instance—and is called upon by the editor to write a story. A contributing editor can also be listed on the masthead as a field correspondent or stringer.

> A contributing editor has a certain expertise that is relevant to a particular interest.

THE ART DIRECTOR AND DESIGNER

The art director gives the magazine its visual style and overall look. Along with the editor, he selects the appropriate type styles (or fonts) for the department and feature story headlines, as well as for body and caption text. The art director also designs the look of each editorial department in the magazine, and oversees the layout of the various feature articles. For the health and look of a magazine, it is important that the edi-

It is important that the editor and art director have a good working relationship.

tor and art director have a good working relationship. Although the editor should have the final say on how an article is presented, at many publishing houses this is not the case.

In multi-title publishing companies, you might see the title "designer" on a masthead. A magazine designer is usually a corporate art director who designs the original look of a magazine so that it has a look and feel similar to the other magazines in the company. Typically, the designer will then step away from the day-to-day responsibilities and allow an art director to interpret his vision.

OTHER POSITIONS

In addition to the positions described above, there are other staff positions that fall within the editorial department. These include fact checkers, who corroborate what the staff has written; photographers, both staff and freelance, who supply photographs for stories; photo editors, who pore over and decide what photographs are worthy of publication; and reporters and field correspondents, who file stories from the field.

6

AN INSIDE LOOK: THE PRODUCTION SIDE OF MAGAZINE PUBLISHING

In this chapter we take a look at the responsibilities of the production department, most often comprised of a production manager and several assistants. The production manager is the person in charge of manufacturing the magazine. In corporate publishing environments, the title is usually the director of manufacturing. Because the production department coordinates many tasks among every discipline of the publishing operation, we'll analyze its duties accordingly.

THE PRODUCTION DEPARTMENT'S ADMINISTRATIVE ROLE

When a magazine is being planned for publication, the production manager is the person responsible for pricing out how much it will cost to produce. The production manager coordinates this pricing with a printer and various other pre-press vendors. The considerations that influence price include paper quality, how much color will be in the magazine, the number of pages, the binding method, the press run (how many copies will be printed) and the freight costs to ship the magazine. There can be others costs, but these are the basics.

Once the magazine has been given a "go" it is then up to the production manager to work up a production schedule. A production schedule is a series of deadline dates that lead up to the newsstand or mail date of the magazine. The produc-

> The production manager is the person in charge of manufacturing the magazine.

The production department makes sure that every department meets its deadline.

tion schedule includes deadlines for the editorial department, the art department, the circulation department and the advertising sales department. It is very important that each department meet these deadlines as the magazine moves along to its print date. The production department makes sure that every department meets its deadline. For a single-title publisher, this task is relatively straightforward. But for a multi-title publisher, where personnel are working on more than one magazine (which is more the norm these days), coordinating work schedules that conform to newsstand and mail dates can get very tricky. The challenge the production department has, therefore, is to efficiently coordinate each magazine's work flow internally to meet the magazine's publication dates.

The publishing date that is the most important is the date when the magazine is shipped to the printer. By that date every editorial lay-out has been approved, every advertiser has been accounted for, newsstand allotments have been finalized (for consumer magazines) and mailing labels for new or renewed subscribers have been updated by the circulation department. After the presses roll, the magazine is shipped and it is on its way to the newsstand and the subscribers. It is standard procedure that as the production department oversees the printing of one issue, they coordinate the production of the next issue at the same time.

As an issue is being put together, the production manager oversees the trafficking and reproduction quality of every page that goes into the magazine. He works with pre-press vendors who produce the pages of the magazine. The production manager also decides—usually with the publisher's approval—how many total pages an issue will be. Generally, this decision is based on the number of advertising pages sold as well as several other considerations.

Without getting into too detailed a discussion on production technology, how and in what configuration the paper for these pages is ordered plays a critical role in determining costs. A savvy production manager can save his publisher literally thousands of dollars by efficiently composing the magazine. Conversely, a production manager who is not diligent can cost the publisher money. Beyond these administrative responsibilities, the production manager works very closely with all the other departments as well.

A savvy production manager can save his publisher thousands of dollars.

THE PRODUCTION DEPARTMENT'S ROLE WITH THE EDITORIAL AND ART DEPARTMENTS

When a production manager is trafficking work produced from the editorial and art departments—like an editorial layout, for instance—the production manager (along with the editor and art director) checks the pages for a variety of elements. These usually include photo reproduction, type alignment, bleed (when the story layout "bleeds," its design goes to the edge of a page) and many other considerations. It is incumbent on the production manager that all these elements be corrected—if not on the first, then on the final proofs. If any mistake is missed, it will be printed in the magazine

79

> **The keen production manager evaluates the layout technically—assessing how well it will print.**

When the keen production manager assesses each layout, he keeps in mind the strengths and weaknesses of the company's printer. He evaluates the layout technically—assessing how well it will print and determining if there will be any potential problems. In this sense, his assessment of editorial layouts is different from that of the art director and editor, both of whom are evaluating the layout for good design and readability. A production manager with a good eye is worth his weight in gold. Like everything else in life, it takes many years of experience to develop a very critical eye.

Moreover, if the editorial or art departments begin to run behind schedule, the production manager will step in and advise them to speed things up. Usually, a good production manager will design a production schedule with a few days of built-in cushion time. This cushion time accommodates such lateness. Sometimes, however, due to a variety of reasons, the editorial or art department will fall perilously behind. It's the production manager who will exhort (sometimes quite vociferously!) each department to get things back on schedule to meet the print date.

THE PRODUCTION DEPARTMENT'S ROLE WITH THE ADVERTISING AND CIRCULATION DEPARTMENTS

During the course of putting together an issue, the production people also work closely with the advertising department. There are several tasks that the production department coordinates with advertising personnel.

As stated before, the production manager

schedules advertising space closing and advertising material deadlines when he creates the production schedule. These dates are used by the advertising department as time frames to sell advertising in each issue. An advertising closing date is the deadline for advertising orders, and the material date is the deadline advertisers must have their advertising materials in the publisher's hand.

When this material arrives at the publishing company's office, the production department receives it, logs it in and then evaluates it for printing. Most advertising material is generally in the form of a piece of negative film called final film, though it can arrive in a variety of forms. If it arrives as final film, the production manager checks that each piece of film conforms with the exact size specifications that the magazine demands. Other specifications—elements with technical terms like line screen, density, register, reading and emulsion—are critical for good reproductive quality, too. If the advertising material that has been sent in is not final film, the production department must transform it into final film. Because it is labor intensive, creating final film from an advertiser's raw material is not usually a task that most production departments would care to do. Nevertheless, save for a very few publishing companies, most magazines perform this service (usually for a fee) for their advertisers.

Production managers are also in charge of pricing out unusual advertising. Often, advertisers want to do something special that stands out in an issue. Ideas can range from a bind-in post-

Production managers are in charge of pricing out unusual advertising.

A strong production team keeps things moving efficiently and economically.

card or a double gatefold to a scented insert or polybagged outsert. The production manager must then determine the extra costs involved in producing such advertising, and advise the advertising director of these extra production costs. The advertising director, in turn, considers these costs when he quotes a price to the advertiser.

In addition to his role with art, editorial and advertising, the production manager also works closely with the circulation department. Specifically, the production manager must get updated subscriber galley counts from the circulation director, as well as newsstand allotments for the various avenues to which the magazine is distributed. Once the production manger knows these exact counts, he writes them on his print order sheet, which is then mailed, faxed or e-mailed to the magazine's printer.

As you can well appreciate by now, the production department plays a critical role in the publishing process. A strong production team keeps things moving efficiently and economically. They play a crucial role in keeping magazine manufacturing costs to a minimum, while at the same time keeping an eye on quality. Not only are they coordinating the work of their colleagues in the publishing company, they are constantly doing quality checks on the printer and pre-press vendors. They are doing all these things while also coordinating all the responsibilities outlined above.

Like everyone else in publishing, production people work under extreme pressure. Unlike some of their editorial or advertising sales colleagues, who are usually deemed the "stars" of the publishing company, production people usually don't get the credit they deserve. It seems that attention is drawn to the production department only when something goes wrong. Yet when everything is running smoothly no one takes notice or stops by to pat them on the back. It's this type of challenge that makes magazine production such a demanding, yet rewarding publishing career.

7

VENDORS SERVICING THE MAGAZINE PUBLISHER

As your knowledge of magazine publishing grows, so too will the realization that not everything it takes to publish magazines is done under the publisher's roof. To broaden your knowledge as you embark upon a career in magazine publishing, you should have an awareness and an understanding of the variety of companies (or vendors) that service the magazine publisher. These companies handle tasks and oversee procedures that the publisher wishes to outsource or are beyond the publisher's expertise. They are in addition to the traditional vendors that any company would need—law firms, accountants, personnel agencies, etc.

Some vendors play a key part in magazine publishing, and their performance can be the difference between success and failure for a magazine publisher. Just like the various departments in a publishing company, most of these companies are task-specific. The following list of vendors is categorized by the magazine publishing department they serve.

> **Not everything it takes to publish magazines is done under the publisher's roof.**

GENERAL MANAGEMENT AND ADVERTISING SALES

Ad Tracking Companies: These companies provide competitive share of market statistics, share of advertiser dollar statistics and other pertinent information to help the advertising sales staff.

85

Some vendors play a key part in magazine publishing.

Collection Companies: Collection companies provide all types of services beyond collecting money from accounts who are in arrears.

Database Marketing Companies: These companies consult with the magazine publisher in setting up a customer base profile to help the publisher cross-sell or upsell its products to existing readership.

Financing Companies: Companies who counsel magazine companies in account receivable financing and investment banking, and assist in securing short- and long-term credit lines.

Management and Marketing Consultants: These companies advise magazine companies—especially new start-up magazine companies—in the overall magazine operation. Services can include editorial positioning, publication design, print production, circulation development, advertising management, contract negotiations, cost-containment strategies and promoting the magazine in the market.

Media Kit and Promotion Companies: These firms help the publisher in the design, implementation and printing of the publisher's promotional materials.

Merger and Acquisition Specialists: Investment banking firms specializing in the publishing and media businesses who broker company mergers or acquisitions.

Publisher's Rep Firms: Independent sales agents who are retained by the magazine publisher to sell advertising for the company's publications.

Research Firms: Market research companies are commissioned by a magazine publisher to analyze and profile a magazine's readership, usually through a combination of qualitative and quantitative research.

CIRCULATION

Alternate Delivery Services: Companies who deliver magazines to subscribers through private delivery rather than using the post office.

Auditing Services: Companies who conduct circulation audits for their member publications to validate a magazine's readership.

Circulation Consultants (Direct Mail): Consultancies who work with magazine companies in their direct mail campaigns. Services include subscription development strategies for new subscription promotion, renewal campaigns, gift subscriptions, copywriting and design of direct mail packages, price and premium testing, modeling and a variety of other services.

Distribution Companies: Companies contracted by the magazine publisher to distribute its magazines. These companies may include a national newsstand distributor, a bookstore distributor, an international distributor, a college bookstore, a computer store, a video store or any other specialty retail account distributor.

Fulfillment Companies: A company who services and maintains the readership file of a magazine or magazine company. There are a slew of services a fulfillment company provides. Some include mailing invoices to new readers, mailing renewal notices to expiring readers, assisting in the preparation of audit services, promotional file maintenance, sales literature fulfillment, pro-

87

cessing reader response cards, product and premium fulfillment and many other services.

List Brokers: Companies who will locate the most responsive, cost-effective mailing list for a magazine company to use for a subscription promotion campaign.

Newsstand Consultants: Companies who counsel magazine publishers on newsstand sales distribution. Services include increasing newsstand sales efficiency, analyzing category title performance, analyzing more efficient distribution channels, conceiving newsstand promotions, and a variety of other services.

Subscription Agencies: These companies supplement the magazine company's DTP (Direct To Publisher) subscription efforts through a variety of programs. The two most well-known subscription agencies are Publishers Clearing House and American Family Enterprises. Subscription agencies cultivate new subscriptions through sweepstakes, school and library catalogs, telemarketing and other sources.

Telephone Marketing Firms: These companies provide inbound and outbound telemarketing services for the magazine publisher. Essentially call centers operating 24 hours a day, seven days a week, their services include order taking, processing change of addresses, new and renewal subscription promotion, direct mail follow-up, circulation audits and surveys.

EDITORIAL, PRODUCTION AND ART

Design Firms: A design firm offers art and design services to magazine publishers for any number of projects, including redesigning an existing publication, or designing a start-up, a special editorial section, an extra supplement or a newsstand special.

Editorial Consultants: These companies provide services that include editorial strategic positioning, training editorial basics to staff, assessing editorial strengths and weaknesses, conducting reader focus studies and providing editorial competitive analyses.

Magazine Printers: Printers, like magazines, come in all shapes and sizes. There are small, medium and long-run magazine printers. Printers print and bind a publisher's magazines as well as provide distribution services. Printers can also provide pre-press services as well as purchase paper for the magazine publisher. In addition to the printer who prints the magazine, a magazine publisher will do business with specialty printers as well. These printers specialize in printing subscription cards, promotional material, inserts, business forms, direct mail packages, booklets, packages and other printed material.

Paper Merchants and Manufacturers: These companies supply paper to the magazine publisher. Merchants (or brokers) offer purchasing services to the magazine publisher for cost-effective paper sourcing.

Pre-press and Composition Services: These companies prepare film for the printing process. Generally, services provided by pre-press houses include stripping, color separation, proofing, digital imaging, archiving, photo manipulation and computer-to-plate services.

Reprint Services: These companies reprint arti-

> **Printers can provide pre-press services as well as purchase paper for the publisher.**

89

cles, advertising sections, etc. from back issues or special issues for the magazine publisher.

Stock Photo Agencies: Archival photo companies who inventory and license photographs, stills and drawings to magazines for publication.

ELECTRONIC PUBLISHING SERVICES

Auditing Services: These companies audit website activity, including page impressions and visits, frequently requested pages or directories, ad impressions and click-through traffic.

Broadcast Fax Companies: Companies who are equipped to provide computerized fax services that include qualifying readers for trade magazines, broadcast faxing of newsletters, subscription promotions and renewals, advertising sales promotion and other services.

CD-ROM Companies: These companies reformat or repurpose printed content into a CD-ROM format. Examples are directories, buying guides and catalogs.

Internet Services: There are a broad range of internet service companies at the magazine publisher's disposal. These include web site development companies, design firms, and companies who provide hosting, programming and on-line commerce capabilities. There are also companies who specialize in updating and maintaining web sites or repurposing printed content into a web format.

> Some vendors can be the difference between success and failure for a publisher.

8

THE COMPUTER AND
THE MAGAZINE PUBLISHER

There was a time not too long ago when magazines were published using instruments called T-squares, triangles, rubies, French curves and typewriters (remember those?). But when the computer invaded the publishing industry, these tools were quickly put aside, packed away into a mythic time capsule that generations from now will look back upon—much like we now fondly recall the wagon wheel.

In most companies today, magazines are created, revised, edited, designed, promoted and marketed on a computer screen. The advertising sales representative traveling in Chicago faxes or e-mails an advertising order to his headquarters in New York using a laptop computer. A production manager instantly analyzes color positioning or page counts for any future issue on his desktop. The circulation staff searches subscription databases right at their desks. The list goes on, but the point is the way the magazine industry does business today is light-years ahead of the way things were done just five years ago. In fact, with the emergence of even newer technology on the horizon, publishing executives will be reinventing their business practices and products for many years to come.

Most magazine publishing companies today are computer-driven. Unbelievably, there are still some publishing companies doing it the old way, using the above-mentioned relics of the past.

Most magazine publishing companies today are computer-driven.

The magazine business today is much faster, more precise and incredibly more flexible.

And unfortunately, it shows. It's manifested in the magazines they produce and the service they provide their customers. When the computer arrived on the publishing scene, there were many naysayers who cried that the publishing industry would never be the same. They declared that the only way to handsomely design and intellectually edit a magazine was by hand. Any other way beyond designing a layout with a triangle or editing text using a blue pencil was verboten. The success of today's technology has kicked those old fogies aside. With the advent of new and improved publishing programs, the magazine business today is much faster, more precise and incredibly more flexible.

The following are brief synopses detailing how the various departments of the publishing business have been revolutionized by the computer. They will also give you a good understanding of the daily work flow and minutiae of the business. They will show you how you might apply your particular computer skills to magazine publishing.

THE EDITORIAL DEPARTMENT

Today's editors receive and edit manuscripts in basically two formats: on computer disk, or through a modem. Unless you are a famous author set in your ways, (and there are a few of those), submitting a paper manuscript is about as acceptable as wearing a brown tie with a black tuxedo. Precious time is wasted having an editorial assistant keystroke an entire paper manuscript into a computer, or having an assistant scan the manuscript into the system. Paper manuscripts slow down the process. And the last thing an editor wants is to slow down the process. As discussed, most editors work at breakneck speed, juggling dozens of tasks throughout the day. They face deadlines constantly. Deadlines for color pages. Deadlines for black and white pages, etc. So if a manuscript comes in on paper, an editor is apt to melt down. Many magazine publishers use Macs and Mac-based programs as their tools of choice, although the market share for PCs has increased over the years. So if your inclination is to break into editing in some capacity, chances are you'll be asked to write and edit on a Mac. And more than likely you'll be asked to edit and write in Microsoft Word.

You might also be asked to write or edit material for the web. Many magazines upload to their web sites a part of their editorial from an on-sale issue as a teaser for potential readers. Indeed, some magazines are already putting up supplements, buyer's guides, and other special issues spun from the core franchise.

Chances are you'll be asked to write and edit on a Mac.

THE ADVERTISING SALES DEPARTMENT

Many magazine publishers keep a computer database of companies who are currently advertising, have advertised or may advertise in the future. From this database advertising sales executives can log an up-to-the-minute diary on their account list. They can key in and have at their fingertips all kinds of information. Some of this information can include basics like the contact name, details of conversations and other logistical information. There might also be information that details present and past contract analy-

> **Gone are the days of dog eared index cards and three-ring binders.**

sis, market share analysis that compares an advertiser's expenditures in their magazine versus the competition, and programs that wave red flags to advise the sales executive when his account is running late on payment. Gone are the days of dog eared index cards and three-ring binders that were the advertising sales modus operandi prior to the computer.

Media kits are promotion packages that advertising sales executives use to tell a prospective advertiser about their magazine. Media kits usually contain information that includes readership demographics and psychographics, advertising rates and other pertinent information. Some publishers support their traditional printed media kit with a CD-ROM presentation. In years past, presentations to clients or advertising agencies were done with flip charts, slides and bar graphs. Today's advertising sales executives use videos, CD-ROMs and the internet as ways of selling advertising space for their magazines.

THE CIRCULATION DEPARTMENT

Circulation directors are a wonderfully diverse lot. Part marketing gurus and part financial mavens, circulators divide their time between studying, forecasting and analyzing data or dreaming up promotion campaigns that will generate more readers. In many ways, the circulation department in past years was ahead of its time. While the rest of the publishing industry was using relics to get their work done, circulation people were using computer technology. Today, the sophistication of the circulation department has become even greater. Need to sort a subscription file by 10 variables? No problem; just give a circulation director a bit of time, and he'll have a report on your desk. Want to forecast a net return on a recent direct mail effort? The CD will run a model to see what the publisher can expect.

In addition to their never-ending quest of finding new readers, renewing existing readers and coming up with razzle-dazzle ideas to win back former readers, circulation directors are also called upon to track and promote ancillary sales generated from items ranging from logo coffee mugs to special issues. Their world is testing new promotion packages, compiling strong mailing lists, launching profitable roll-outs and netting a pay-up that keeps their magazines afloat. And they do all of their prospecting, figuring and modeling with state-of-the-art computer spreadsheets and modeling analysis. Lots of publishers use Excel, or custom-design a program to meet their specific needs.

Circulation directors do all of their prospecting with computer spreadsheets and modeling analysis.

High-tech marketing strategies usually are outgrowths of the circulation and advertising departments. They include database marketing, which lets the publisher tailor editorial and advertising content to special segments of a readership. Selective binding allows publishers to customize special editions to targeted subscribers. Ink jet imaging lets publishers and advertisers print personalized messages to subscribers. And finally, with the aid of high-tech printing technology, there are reader involvement devices like scent strips, musical inserts and pop-up advertising. And let's not forget how circulation directors now use the internet as a market-

The production department is the hub of the publishing wheel.

ing tool. On many magazine sites, you can subscribe or renew your subscription, change your address, order back issues, or inquire about when your subscription will expire. Some magazines are also offering reader service programs so that advertisers can send them free information.

On the newsstand side of circulation, the computer is used in a variety of ways. Sample applications include profiling a magazine's market share against its category competitors in cities (or select cities) around the country; analyzing overall domestic, Canadian and foreign sales on a weekly basis; and wholesaler and retail applications that include tracking a magazine's sell-through efficiencies. An evolving retailer application, Pay-On-Scan (another term that's being used is Scan Based Trading) is scanning a magazine's UPC (Universal Product Code). This point of sale scanning technology lets the retailer determine sales by magazine title, category, SKU (stock-keeping unit) number, time and price—as well as other more detailed information.

THE PRODUCTION DEPARTMENT

It's been said that the production department is the hub of the publishing wheel. The production department coordinates the work flow that emanates from the editorial, art, sales and circulation departments. Without the production manager keeping things running on time, there would be chaos. One of the most important elements in a production manager's life is the calendar. He coordinates the various deadlines with the printer and other vendors. Determining deadlines can be a daunting task if a production manager is overseeing a multi-title operation, as many are. In the old days, production managers spent half their lives staring at a calendar, counting days, and subtracting weekends and holidays, in their quest to work up a realistic production schedule that was amenable to all departments. Today, computers are used to forecast deadline dates, taking into account a number of variables, including conflicting work schedules between departments.

Production managers also use computers to oversee pre-press work, lay out an issue of a magazine, keep track of advertising materials that are being sent in by advertisers and estimate costs for a particular project the publisher is considering for the future. Publishers over the years have spent a lot of money upgrading the production department. New technology, like CTP (computer-to-plate) workflows, has begun to be embraced by many magazine publishers. Magazine production departments are using telecommunications to connect with the company's printers and pre-press vendors. Production departments also have taken the lead in archiving digital files. And many more pre-press tasks are being performed by the production department, including color corrections, four-color digital proofing and high resolution scanning. The number of digital ads sent in by advertising agencies has also increased. All these production efficiencies will continue to become part of the norm for many, many publishers in the future. The challenge for today's publishers is to have their non-agency advertisers conform to these new formats too.

Today, computers are used to forecast deadline dates.

THE ART DEPARTMENT

Layout changes can be made almost instantly on the screen.

When you walk into a computer-based art department, what you'll most likely see are art directors actually sitting at a desk working in front of a computer. I've stressed sitting because it was not that long ago—and still is the case at some publishers—that most art directors were forced to hunch over a slanted art table, and with plastic triangles, T-squares and French curves in hand, design magazine pages. With the advent of computer technology and the slew of design programs, art directors today can work more efficiently and have more flexibility in designing their layouts. And have a healthier sacroiliac, too!

When an editor reviews layouts with an art director, changes can be made almost instantly on the screen. All kinds of editorial changes are possible: Fonts (type styles) can be changed, color shades can be fine-tuned, and photos can be moved or repositioned, all at the click of a mouse button. The flexibility and exploration of instantaneous creativity is marvelous. For the most part, Macs are the computers of choice for magazine art departments. Design tools most commonly found in a magazine publishing art department include QuarkXPress, Illustrator and Photoshop. As technology improves, other graphic arts tasks will be absorbed by the art department as well, making costs and turnaround time more favorable to the publisher.

FINANCE AND ACCOUNTING

The finance and accounting folks spend a lot of time budgeting, forecasting and modeling a variety of financial information. The computer will run reports on cash flow analysis, accounts receivables, accounts payables, billing, payroll and taxes. Obviously, proficiency with a computer and familiarity with electronic spreadsheets are important for any career in the accounting or financial area. At a large magazine publishing company you might be assigned to one task—keeping track of the paper inventory, or analyzing newsstand cash flow, for instance. Or you might be assigned to work on profit and loss statements for each issue. Whatever task is at hand, chances are you'll be using a computer spreadsheet program, most likely Excel, if you desire a career in magazine finance or accounting.

THE PEOPLE WHO KEEP THE COMPUTERS RUNNING: THE INFORMATION SYSTEMS STAFF

Because of all the computer technology that has invaded the publishing company, the IS staff has evolved into a central part of the magazine publishing operation. As in other industries, Information Systems people are the computer gurus of the magazine company. They are, without question, worth their weight in gold. If the production department is in charge of keeping the trains running on time, the IS staff is in charge of making sure the electricity is turned on. They are the people overseeing all the computer systems in a magazine company, from hardware installation to software purchasing. These folks enjoy the challenge of finding solutions to computer problems. They are wonderfully creative people who speak in a code most of us don't understand.

The IS staff has evolved into a central part of the magazine publishing operation.

An IS staff can make a company work more efficiently and productively. In very small magazine publishing companies, it is common to see the production manager, senior art director or circulation director doubling as the IS guru. Whatever way it is structured, the magazine publisher who is serious about its business should have an IS staff, a department that was not that common for the average publisher just a few short years ago.

9

THE ELECTRONIC
PUBLISHING REVOLUTION

Just as the computer has revolutionized the way magazine companies do business operationally, it has also opened new avenues for they way magazine publishing companies deliver information. Over the last decade, we have witnessed an astonishing revolution of how information is delivered to the consumer. With the advent of the CD-ROM, the internet, and other electronic technology, magazine publishing companies today are evolving into multi-media disseminators of information through a variety of outlets. Indeed, when people I meet ask me what business I'm in, I say—slightly tongue in cheek—"I'm in the information dissemination business."

Driven by today's technology, the definition of what a "magazine publisher" is has taken on a variety of meanings. Indeed, the revolution of "repurposing content"—taking what you have on the printed page and formatting it for the web or other electronic media—has created new career opportunities in magazine publishing. Job titles that years before hadn't existed, like web editor or electronic information director, have sprouted up on many a magazine's masthead. What this translates to for today's job seeker is a broader range of career opportunities in magazine publishing. As the publishing industry continues to evolve and redefine itself, these career opportunities will certainly abound. Let's explore the various formats of electronic publishing

"I'm in the information dissemination business."

found in the traditional magazine publishing environment.

THE INTERNET

> The key to any well-designed web site is to keep its material fresh.

The internet has become a limitless marketplace of information, entertainment, products and services. Most industry experts acknowledge that magazine publishers need to have a presence on the web—if for no other reason than the very nature of the business they are in. Indeed, magazine publishers are ideal content providers, because they are already in the content-providing business. Many magazine publishers use the internet as a cross-marketing and promotional tool to promote their magazine line to both present and potential readers. The key, of course, to any well-designed web site is to keep its material fresh. Magazine publishers keep their sites fresh with the same steady flow of information they feed their print readers with every new issue.

Yet there are basic nuances of publishing on the net and other electronic formats that are much different from magazine publishing. I once asked an editor of one of the magazines I was publishing to move over to the internet and become our company's web editor. To say that he flourished is an understatement. In short, he did a great job, not only with the internet but with several other electronic projects. He was able to successfully adapt his solid editorial sensibilities to electronic formats. He quickly grasped that each medium he worked within offered different ways of delivering information. And he took advantage of each format's possibilities. How was he able to do that? He understood that while the basic

106

underlying foundation of delivering quality editorial was still key, the dynamics of delivering information were different from format to format.

So while there are wonderful tools at your disposal as you edit on the web—sound, chat rooms, animation, etc.—you must first have quality content that changes often to create a well-trafficked, successful web site. You might recall what I mentioned in Chapter 1. Publishing, in any format, is an ongoing conversation between an editor and his staff and their readers (or users). If the conversation gets stale, readership (or traffic) will erode precipitously.

Successful web editors understand that editing on the web involves taking full advantage of the available technology to create a web site that is a living, breathing information delivery system. Hyperlinking (connecting to other pages within or outside a site), animation, chat rooms, video and audio all make a web site dynamic and interactive. Successful editors make the most of the web medium. They also understand that there are logical considerations that must be addressed when adapting an article from a printed magazine onto the web. Jump lines (directions to readers to turn to another page in the magazine) and date references, for instance, must all be edited out to give the article immediacy in the web format.

Successful web page designers who work within the magazine industry understand there are differences in format design for them as well. The successful web designer will acknowledge that the number one priority when designing on the web is the size of the file that is created. How fast will the file download? A highly stylized web design

Quality content that changes often creates a well-trafficked, successful web site.

Good web design lets the user move around the site with the least amount of effort.

that takes too long to download will frustrate users. Successful designers meet this challenge. Color selection and the amount of graphics, for instance, are two elements that affect download speed.

Font size must be addressed because fonts on most PCs are larger than on Macs. Page size—static in the magazine environment—changes on the web. Page composition is different too. Once a designer learns how to adapt to these elements of design, he must then create an easy-to-use site. Furthermore, unlike the magazine format, where all the reader is asked to do is read content and turn a page, web design asks users to navigate a site. Designers must develop what is known as a graphic user interface to get the user to move around a site. Good web design lets the user move around the site with the least amount of effort or, optimally, without even thinking. The navigation becomes unconscious, as unconscious as turning a printed page. Graphic user interface is not a new concept. Indeed, one book several successful web designers recommend for the aspiring web designer is *The Design of Everyday Things* by Donald Norman. The book discusses how design automatically inspires function. Design challenges that exist on the web are more sophisticated than those found in the magazine format.

If you wish to work as an editor or designer on the web, a good start is to learn HTML—Hyper Text Mark-Up Language. HTML is a very simple mark-up language. There are books and web sites available on HTML that will teach you this language. There is also software—PageMill, Dreamweaver and Front Page—known as WYSIWYG (What You See Is What You Get) software that will write HTML for you as you format your text. Once the text is laid in, images to accompany the text must be scanned for the web design format. The images are then converted to either a GIF or JPEG file format to be placed into the text. It is then a matter of "cutting and pasting" the photos into the text. For designers wishing to work on the web there are several programs to learn. These include BBEdit, Debabelizer and Notepad. You should already know Photoshop. So if you have a strong technical understanding of the internet mixed with strong editorial or artistic sensibilities, the internet may be for you.

What has evolved over the years is the trend toward a team concept in web design. When the web first came along, a web master—an all-in-one employee—was in charge of a company's site Today, the responsibilities, much like the magazine staff, are departmentalized. Teams comprised of editors, designers, technical people and sales and marketing personnel support a company's web site. While the sales and marketing people are selling banners, links or sponsorship programs (those of you in sales should check selling on the web—there are lots of opportunities available!) the techies are searching for new software and the editors and designers are creating new pages.

The trend is toward a team concept in web design.

CD-ROMS

In the 1990s, CD-ROMs made the leap from the library shelf to the consumer marketplace. Because of their capacity to store a tremendous amount of information in a small format, CD-

CD-ROM projects embrace a variety of positions, similar to the hierarchy of a magazine.

ROMs were the perfect archival tool for libraries. But now their role has been expanded and redefined. Over the last several years, CD-ROMs have taken off in the consumer marketplace. Initially much of their use was through business applications like sales and marketing presentations. Today, the diversity of CD-ROM reference, entertainment and educational titles is as broad as that of books.

The added element that CD-ROMs bring to the marketplace which books cannot is their interactivity. You can spend hours exploring the seemingly limitless excursions of a CD-ROM. As prices continue to drop and CD-ROM drives became more prevalent in the marketplace, the use of CD-ROMs will increase exponentially.

Today's publishers are using CD-ROMs in different ways. In addition to publishing original material on CD-ROMs, many are drawing on their backlists or archival material to package previously published material in a dynamic new environment. For publishers who can't afford to set up a CD-ROM operation, a partnership with a CD-ROM developer is an option. Nevertheless, regardless of how high tech the technology might be, the bottom line to a quality CD-ROM is its content. Just like a high-quality magazine or a good book, a high-quality, content-rich CD-ROM will have a long shelf life.

Career opportunities on CD-ROM projects embrace a variety of positions, similar to the hierarchy of a magazine. Like the publisher of a magazine, the CD-ROM publisher is the person who has final say on what the budget will be for a specific project. Reporting to the publisher are title managers or producers, who function much like an editor-in-chief, and who will select the appropriate editor to shape the material.

Rounding out the team usually is a line producer or developer, who is the technical person on the project, and an art director, who handles the art and design. There are, of course, researchers, associate editors and other support personnel on a CD-ROM project as well.

There are several basic steps to producing a CD-ROM. The first step is to draft a comprehensive outline detailing what information will be presented. Next is to actually compile an exhaustive repository of information. This information is usually in the form of text, photography, audio and video. And the final step is to program this information onto a master CD-ROM disk.

30% of the budget for CD-ROM titles typically is dedicated to sales and marketing.

While the product is being created by the editorial people, the sales and marketing department—usually spearheaded by the publisher—is working to develop an attractive package design and set up distribution avenues. Because of fierce competition among CD-ROM titles, 30% of the budget typically is dedicated to sales and marketing. While CD-ROMs are found in bookstores, the majority of CD-ROMs are sold through computer stores and mail order. Not surprisingly, game titles account for the bulk sales of the industry's market—industry experts estimate anywhere from 50-80% of the total share. Fast-growing categories include productivity and home office titles. Successful CD-ROM development requires the same essential elements as that of publishing a successful magazine. Editors must have a great sensibility for the subject, possess a

Audio tapes and videos play a major role in electronic publishing.

keen eye for detail and be passionate about the subject. Art directors must fully understand the CD-ROM medium and know how to adopt their design sensibilities to an interactive environment. And line producers, much like production people in magazines, must integrate all the processes. Some basic work tools for editors, line producers and artists when developing a CD-ROM include software such as DeBabelizer (multimedia graphics software), Premiere (digital video software), Director (multimedia authoring software), Page-Maker and Illustrator (graphics software), Sound Designer (audio software) and Digital Performer (music and audio effects sequencing software). Highly sophisticated CD-ROMs will demand their own programming. And once the final product is completed, publishers and sales and marketing people must aggressively and smartly position it in the marketplace to optimize sales.

AUDIO TAPES AND VIDEO TECHNOLOGY

When publishing people talk about electronic publishing, many get so caught up in the romance and technospeak of the web and CD-ROMs that they never get around to exploring the viability of audio tapes and videos as publishing formats. In fact, audio tapes and videos play a major role in electronic publishing—the next time you are in your favorite mega-bookstore, notice the large amount of display space dedicated to audio tapes and videos.

Much printed content can be replicated in an audio format—either abridged or unabridged. Or original material can be produced direct to audio tape. At a magazine company I oversaw, we developed a highly successful and highly profitable series of audio tapes using popular material from printed content. The career opportunities available here include script writers, voice-over talent and sound engineers. And let's not forget the art director's role in designing the packaging, or the sales and marketing director's expertise in getting the tape promoted and distributed.

Video production is a more expensive publishing format, but with today's technology, it's not out of the realm for most magazine publishers' budgets. Producing a successful video is a highly labor-intensive business that demands the talents of a number of people, including a screenwriter, producer, camera operator, director, video editor, on-screen talent, voice-over talent, animators, art directors, and sales and marketing people. Most magazine publishers who produce videos generally avoid all the work of developing a video production unit and easily contract a video production house that works jointly with them to produce a project.

A small number of publishers—I was one!—are crazy enough to create a video production unit and produce videos in-house. A sizable investment in equipment and staff is needed, but the creative juices really flow when you can successfully marry the staff of a magazine with the staff of a video production unit.

If publishing in any of these—the internet, CD-ROMs, audio or video— inspires you as you explore the traditional magazine discipline, check out publishers who are delivering content in these formats. There are, of course, a plethora of

Opportunities available in video production include script writers, voice-over talent and sound engineers.

other companies who are disseminating information through electronic media as well.

To learn more about the electronic publishing business, the following is a resource directory of trade magazines, trade fairs, and URLs that you should check out.

Check out publishers who are delivering content through the internet, CD-ROMs, audio or video.

TRADE MAGAZINES

Digital Video
411 Borel Avenue, Ste. 100
San Mateo, CA 94402
Tel: (650) 358-9500
Written for professionals involved in digital video production, post-production or delivery.

Electronic Media
740 N. Rush Street
Chicago, IL 60611
Tel: (312) 649-5200
Edited for the management of broadcast, television, cable, audio and related media technologies.

eMagazineweekly (formerly MacWeek)
301 Howard Street
San Francisco, CA 94105
Tel: (415) 243-3500
A newsweekly dedicated to the needs of digital media managers.

Internet World
20 Ketchum Street
Westport, CT 06880
Tel: (203) 226-6967
www.iw.com

For the internet professional covering topics
such as internet business strategy, technical
implementation, programming and design.

InternetWeek
600 Community Drive
Manhasset, NY 11030
Tel: (516) 562-5549
www.interwk.com
Addresses the information needs of network/IS
professionals and corporate management.

Inter@ctive Week
100 Quentin Roosevelt Blvd.
Garden City, NY 11530
Tel: (516) 229-3700
www.zd.com/intweek/
Edited for the IS decision maker and focusing
on business and technical issues in creating
internet and intranet applications.

Journal of the Audio Engineering Society
60 East 42nd Street
New York, NY 10165-2520
Tel: (212) 661-2355
Written for technical audio professionals includ-
ing audio engineers and audio technicians.

MultiMedia Systems Design
575 Market Street, Ste. 500
San Francisco, CA 94105
Tel: (415) 278-5302
Targeted to professionals developing the hardware and software for audio, video and graphics
for consumer and computer applications.

115

Video and MultiMedia Producer
701 Westchester Avenue
White Plains, NY 10604
Tel: (914) 328-9157
For creative professionals in video and
multimedia design.

Video Systems
9800 Metcalf
Overland Park, KS 66212-2215
Tel: (913) 341-1300
Written for video professionals working at
independent production facilities or corporate
video workplaces.

WEBTechniques
411 Borel Avenue, Ste. 100
San Mateo, CA 94402
Tel: (650) 655-4194
www.webtechniques.com
Provides technical expertise for the web
professional planning, building and managing
web sites.

TRADE SHOWS

AIIM
Information & Image Management Exhibit
AIIM International
1100 Wayne Avenue,Suite. 1100
Silver Spring, MD 20910
Tel: (301) 587-8202
Annual marketplace for equipment, supplies
and services for the information and document
management industry.

Audio Engineering Society Convention
60 East 42nd Street
New York, NY 10165
Tel: (212) 661-8525
An annual marketplace for professional audio
equipment professionals.

COMDEX
300 First Avenue
Needham, MA 02194
Tel: (617) 433-1500
For the computer industry's independent resell-
ers of computer systems and related products.

Computer Game Developers' Conference
600 Harrison Street
San Francisco, CA 94107
Tel: 800-227-2675
Conference and trade show dedicated to devel-
opers of interactive digital entertainment.

Digital Video Conference and Exposition
525 Market Street, Ste. 500
San Francisco, CA 94195
Tel: (415) 278-5300
Conference for working video professionals
using or wanting to learn about digital video.

Electronic Entertainment Expo (E3)
1400 Providence Hwy.
Norwood, MA 020262
Tel: (617) 551-9800
E3 is focused on interactive entertainment and
educational products that cover leisure time
digital interests.

Internet World
20 Ketchum Street
Westport, CT 06880
Tel: (203) 226-6967
Showcase for the tools, talent and technology
driving the success of the internet.

International Winter
Consumer Electronics Show
2500 Wilson Blvd.
Arlington, VA 22201-3834
Tel: (703) 907-7600
Serves as the showcase dedicated solely to
consumer electronics products.

MultiCom
2032 Virginia Avenue
McLean, VA 22101-4940
Tel: (703) 536-2100
Annual meeting and exposition for printing and
related graphic arts services.

On Demand Digital Printing & Publishing
Strategy Conference and Exposition
363 Reef Road
Fairfield, CT 06430-0915
Tel: (203) 256-4700
On Demand provides a forum for buyers and
sellers of digital printing and publishing equip-
ment, software and services.

PC Expo
One Penn Plaza
New York, NY 10119
Tel: (212) 714-1300

International broad-based computer show
encompassing computer hardware, software,
portable computing, multimedia, electronic
publishing and other applications.

Photo Marketing Association International
3000 Picture Place
Jackson, MI 49201
Tel: (517) 788-8100
Serves the picture taking and picture processing
needs of consumer, professional and graphic and
business markets.

Seybold Seminars
303 Vintage Park Drive
Foster City, CA 94404-1138
Tel: (415) 578-6900
Seybold brings together publishing, graphics
and printing professionals to discuss topics such
as internet publishing, multimedia design, work-
flow automation and color management.

SIGGRAPH
150 Burling Avenue
Clarendon Hills, IL 60514-1203
Tel: (630) 850-7779
SIGGRAPH provides an annual marketplace for
computer graphics equipment and services.

Software Development
600 Harrison Street
San Francisco, CA 94107
Tel: (800) 227-4675
Software Development offers an environment
for technology, transfer and information

119

exchange within the software and application development industry.

Video Software Dealers Association Convention
16530 Ventura Blvd., Ste. 400
Encino, CA 91436
Tel: (818) 385-1500
Provides a forum of communication for the video industry.

Web.X—The Internet Event for Business
One Penn Plaza
New York, NY 10119
Tel: (212) 714-1300
The internet solutions event for businesses of every size. Runs concurrently with PC Expo.

URLs

Browserwatch
A resource about browsers and plug-ins.
http://browserwatch.internet.com

CWS APPS
A list of downloadable Windows applications.
http://cws.internet.com

Internetnews.com
Internet-specific news.
www.internetnews.com

The List
An in-depth directory of internet service providers.
http://thelist.internet.com

Webdeveloper.com
Daily news, product reviews and downloads of interest to web designers, programmers and developers.
www.webdeveloper.com

Webreference.com
An online library of news, advice and how-to articles for those building web sites.
www.webreference.com

10

MAGAZINE PUBLISHING AND THE LAW

B ecause of the nature of the business, magazine publishing has become increasingly exposed to lawsuits over the years. In fact, the number of lawsuits against publishing companies continues to rise. In today's litigious society, this is not surprising. If you plan on making magazine publishing your career, in whatever capacity, it is important that you have a basic understanding of some of the legal entanglements that you or your company might encounter. Here are a few.

DEFAMATION/LIBEL

In short, defamation or libel is something written that injures a person's reputation. While defamation could be an action or incident, most times it is written words that injure the person's esteem or social standing. It can be in the form of a magazine article that ridicules the person in some way; implies the person is incompetent in his trade, occupation or profession; or challenges his corporation's integrity, credit or ability to carry on business.

If you're an editor about to publish an expose or investigative article, it is imperative that it is based on corroborated facts. An article steeped in innuendo, gossip or hearsay will expose you, your magazine and your company to a lawsuit. Too often an inexperienced editor will publish what he thinks is a factual story and then find out

The number of lawsuits against publishing companies continues to rise.

> **If you didn't write the story, you should ask the writer who did several questions.**

later that it is untrue (or cannot be corroborated). If you think you are treading on dangerous ground, then you probably are. At this point, let the company attorney review the article for possible legal liability. This includes anything that you think is potentially libelous: a story, sidebar or related piece, headline, photograph, illustration or graphic.

If you didn't write the story, you should ask the writer who did several questions: Did he have any bias when writing the piece? Did he contact all relevant persons to obtain corroborative information? Did he review all relevant documents? Did he place excessive reliance on biased or inherently unreliable sources? Has he relied exclusively on a confidential source?

A defamation suit can be very costly in terms of money and reputation for the publishing company. In addition to a financial settlement, the publisher might be sanctioned in some way and forced to write a correction or clarification. Especially in today's climate, it's imperative that the writer and editor be prudent before undertaking and/or publishing a provocative story that could be libelous.

INVASION OF PRIVACY

Suppose you're an assistant editor who writes for a trade magazine that reports on the furniture industry. You are asked to interview a company president. During the course of the interview, he mentions that he is a recovering substance abuser. Your story includes his bout with substance abuse, and your editor runs the piece. Several days after the article hits the street, you get a call from the company's lawyers threatening a suit based on invasion of privacy. The lawyers claim that certain parts of the article that dealt with his substance abuse were private and embarrassing facts. Furthermore, these facts are not a legitimate concern of the public. Unless you can produce a written consent or release that was signed by the company president, you and your company are exposed to an invasion of privacy suit.

Invasion of privacy is also manifested by the appropriation of someone's name and/or likeness without prior written consent. Usually this type of invasion of privacy is threatened when a person's name or likeness is used for advertising or trade purposes. Say, for instance, you use someone's photograph to promote your magazine for a subscription campaign, but you didn't secure prior written consent. You are again exposed to an invasion of privacy suit.

Yet another interpretation of invasion of privacy is false light and intrusion. False light is when someone falsely gives publicity to a matter concerning another person that places that person in a false light. In this case, the false light in which the plaintiff was placed would be highly offensive to a reasonable person, or the person giving publicity acted with reckless disregard.

Intrusion is when a person intentionally intrudes, physically or otherwise, upon the solitude or seclusion of another, or his or her private affairs or concerns.

Invasion of privacy is the appropriation of someone's name and/or likeness without prior written consent.

COPYRIGHT AND TRADEMARKS

Copyright is a major issue in the publishing busi-

> **Be very cautious when it comes to using something that might be construed as a copyright infringement.**

ness. When you own the copyright to something that you've written, illustrated or designed, you have the sole right to its use in the future. With that said, however, others can use part of what you've written within what's called "fair use." Fair use means others can use your material in a reasonable manner. What is a reasonable manner? Many times it's what the courts have to decide.

I have always instructed my editors to be very cautious when it comes to using something that might be construed as a copyright infringement. It is better to err on the side of caution than to have a costly copyright lawsuit brought against the company.

A trademark is a word or name that identifies a manufacturer. Magazines can sometimes get into trouble with trademarks if they do a parody or satirical article (or publish a parody advertisement) without the use of an obvious disclaimer attached to the article. When publishing a parody, there absolutely must be no question that the piece presented is indeed a parody. In addition to a disclaimer, the publisher might also want to position the parody in a non-confusing location and/or alter the protected trademark in a significant manner.

PRODUCT LIABILITY

Claims have been brought against magazine publishers who publish "how-to" articles that clearly endorses potentially dangerous endeavors or potentially dangerous products. These can range from exercise routines, weapons, food recipes, or medical advice. Up to the present time, the courts have been reluctant to give credence to such claims, often citing First Amendment concerns.

To avoid as well as defend against product liability claims, it's important that the wise publisher take a few steps. A good practice might be to print a disclaimer stating that the editor's findings are what occurred at the time of the test, and that future tests might yield varying results. For the publisher who prints many product reviews, like *Consumer Reports Magazine*, for example, implementing defensible guidelines for product tests is an advisable start. If freelance writers or outside "experts" are conducting the tests, it's important that the publisher receive verification of all the steps that took place during the test.

One way publishers protect themselves is through liability insurance. Although this type of insurance is expensive, certain insurance policies will cover, with a deductible, product liability suits brought against the publisher. A smart publisher will have such insurance. For even more protection, many publishers ask for and receive indemnification from advertisers or manufacturers of the products that the magazine will be testing.

As you can see, the publishing business is wrought with legal land mines. That's why it is very important to be prudent when disseminating information. Smart publishing people stay abreast of legal developments, trends and legal decisions that might have an impact on them in the future. Hiring a skilled attorney who specializes in matters of media law and setting up guidelines that are always followed will serve to protect the publisher against possible lawsuits.

The publishing business is wrought with legal land mines.

127

11

OPPORTUNITIES BEYOND THE MAGAZINE PUBLISHING COMPANY

What do AT&T, United Airlines and McDonald's have in common? In addition to being leaders in the telecommunication, airline and hamburger businesses, all of them are in the publishing business. In fact, check the company listings on the American and New York Stock Exchanges, as well as NASDAQ. You'll see a whole slew of businesses in the publishing business. How? These companies all publish a corporate report, a yearly synopsis detailing the performance of their company and a vision for future growth. And because there is a staff in charge of producing this report, it stands to reason that a corporate report position is just one publishing opportunity beyond the traditional magazine publishing company. As you begin your job search for a publishing position, keep in mind this "hidden" opportunity that lays beyond the traditional magazine publishing company. Let's take a look at corporate reports as well as other non-traditional publishing disciplines that offer publishing opportunities.

A corporate report position is just one opportunity beyond magazine publishing.

CORPORATE REPORTS

As mandated by the Security Exchange Commission, every publicly held company must publish and distribute a corporate report to its stockholders. Some corporate reports are modest presentations. Others, like those issued by Fortune 500 companies, are sophisticated periodicals that

129

rival (and in many instances surpass) the quality of most magazines.

To reiterate, the corporate report details the performance of the company. And whether the company is going through good times or bad, information always looks better in a high-quality presentation. Corporate reports generally are put together by the company's communication or public relations department, or they are out-sourced to a vendor who produces the report for the company. Those companies that do publish corporate reports in-house are good potential opportunities for the job seeker looking to break into the publishing business. While some of the dynamics are different from the traditional magazine publishing discipline, it's a good way to break-in and learn about the publishing business—especially if you wish to work in editorial or production.

> **Information always looks better in a high-quality presentation.**

HOUSE ORGANS

House organs are publications published for the employees of a company. They can be in the form of a newsletter, magazine or e-mail. Generally house organs are found in large multinational companies. Their frequencies (how many times they are published) vary from monthly to quarterly. IBM's *Think Magazine* is a good example of a house organ. It reports on the activities of the company, including global news, employee and division activities and new developments or products.

In most instances, house organs are published by the company's communications office or human resources department. Depending on the size of the company and the sophistication of the house organ, staff size can range from a one-person operation to a full staff. House organs disseminate everything that is going on in a company, so it's a great way to stay up-to-date on what your company is doing.

CUSTOM PUBLISHERS

Custom publishing has grown rapidly over the last several years. It is a $1 billion industry in the U.S. Custom publishers are firms that specialize in publishing magazines for other companies not in the publishing business. Typically, a custom published magazine is designed as part of the overall marketing strategy by the client company. It's publishing in the service of marketing. Many companies use a custom magazine to form long-term relationships with their target audience. Acura, Home Depot, and Chrysler are just a few companies who have custom magazines. Acura's magazine, called *AcuraDriver,* supplements its main editorial focus—promoting the Acura nameplate—with lifestyle and travel articles. Most inflight magazines found in seat pockets on airlines all over the world are produced by custom publishers. The airline inflight magazine segment alone is a $100 million business. There are also custom published magazines produced for cruise lines, hotels and rail lines.

Usually a custom publisher targets a specific market—health care, for instance—and custom publishes magazines, newsletters, web sites or other media for large companies in that market. Custom publishing can often be contracted out to a traditional publishing company as well.

Custom publishing is a $1 billion industry in the U.S.

131

Many large publishing companies, like Hachette and The New York Times Company, aggressively promote their custom publishing divisions. A custom magazine can also be published by the company's communications office.

INDUSTRY ASSOCIATION MAGAZINES

For every industry, there is an association. And for every association there is some kind of periodical that keeps its members up-to-date on the happenings of the industry. Some association publications are very slick, high-quality magazines, that carry advertising and require a full staff. Others are no more than a two- to three-page newsletter. For a listing of associations in your area, check with your local library. They are a good source for an entry-level publishing opportunity.

> For every association there is some kind of periodical that keeps its members up-to-date.

NONPROFIT FOUNDATIONS AND GOVERNMENT AGENCY OFFICES

Almost every major nonprofit foundation publishes a magazine. Some, like *Arthritis Today*, which is published by the Arthritis Foundation, have evolved into consumer magazines, serving readerships that are quite substantial. Foundation magazines target the issue (or issues) that are the purpose of the foundation.

Federal, state, and local government agencies publish magazines, newsletters, booklets and information sheets on just about everything. Almost every agency at any level of government has a publishing budget. Check with your local or state government office regarding publishing opportunities that might be available.

CATALOGS

Catalog publishing has evolved into an industry unto itself. Most catalogs are published by a full staff similar in nature to a traditional magazine. Practically the same elements found in the traditional publishing process are also part of catalog publishing. I've hired production and graphic arts personnel from the catalog business, and their transition into magazine publishing was seamless.

Keep in mind all these "hidden" publishing disciplines as you search for your magazine publishing opportunity. Target the magazine publishing companies first—but if you come up short, don't ignore these alternative choices as a way to land a publishing position.

Most catalogs are published by a full staff similar to a traditional magazine.

12

SO HOW MUCH CAN YOU EARN?

O kay, so now let's get to the real important stuff. How much money can you make in the magazine business? At what point can you start counting your millions? While the magazine business is certainly a glamorous industry to the layperson, with Hollywood images of richly appointed corner offices in gleaming skyscrapers and sleek limousines adding to the allure, the truth is there are precious few people who make millions editing, selling advertising or marketing a magazine. You can, however, make a very comfortable living. A good rule of thumb is to remember that generally the bigger the company, the higher your compensation package. And if the moment ever moves you, you might want to think about jumping into the entrepreneurial pool and starting your own magazine. If it's successful, the sky's the limit as far as earnings are concerned. But since this book is geared to professional development in the magazine business, let's concentrate on salaries first.

Generally the bigger the company, the higher your compensation package.

Each year, *Folio:Magazine*, the magazine written for magazine professionals, publishes detailed surveys outlining salary levels for editorial, production, art and circulation personnel. A detailed questionnaire is mailed to a large number of magazine professionals working in each discipline of the business. The surveys are mailed twice to increase the response from each discipline. The questions include age, responsibility,

Finding a top-notch editor is one of the hardest searches in publishing.

number of employees supervised (if any), total circulation of the magazine the respondent works on, frequency and total pages produced annually. *Folio:* also categorizes the survey from the highest salary reported to the lowest, as well as the average bonus, if any. The results are further analyzed by region, experience in the business, gender and size of company. If you are interested in obtaining a reprint of any one of *Folio:*'s surveys, call their main office in Stamford, Connecticut at (203) 358-9900 to purchase a copy. So how much can you earn? Let's take a look at the various publishing disciplines.

EDITORIAL AND ART SALARIES

As we discussed earlier, editing a magazine is a 24 hour a day, seven days a week job. Even when editors are out of their offices, their minds are constantly working and churning, thinking up new story ideas to enhance future issues. When I was an editor I kept a notebook and pen on a table near my bed so that I could quickly jot down ideas for magazines (I continue the practice today). You just never know where and at what time of day a great idea will come to mind.

Finding a top-notch editor is one of the hardest searches in publishing. The highly successful editor must be a visionary and at the same time an ambassador for the magazine. The creativity of an editor can sometimes be diametrically opposed to the required business responsibilities. There are many editors who have a terrific vision, yet fail miserably when they are asked to schmooze with advertising clients, or even with their own readers! If you're thinking about an editorial career, you must keep in mind that magazine publishing is a business. The owners are in it to make money. Therefore, if at times you are asked to make nice with a big advertiser over lunch, it would be in your best interest for you to politely acquiesce. If the demands go further, like running "puff" pieces about a large advertiser, then you will have to make the call on just how far you'll go. From experience, however, I can tell you that the most valuable editor is the one who edits a great magazine while at the same time knows how to work a room to promote his magazine.

The average salary for an editor who has four to 10 years experience in the business can range from $44,000 to $52,000. Compensation goes higher as you move up the editorial ladder, especially when you begin managing other editors as an editorial director. And editorial salary levels are generally higher on the east and west coasts. For an entry-level editorial position, salaries can range from $14,000 to $30,000.

Art directors work long hours to create the visual appeal of the magazine, and their work schedule can extend into the wee hours of the night. Why? The art department is the last stop for an 11th hour-article that needs to run in the magazine. Sometimes the editor is late with a story. The responsibility then falls to the art department to get it out the door to make the print deadline. Unfortunately, this means playing catch-up and working around the clock. This is an ongoing phenomenon in the business, and at times it's justified. But I've always disliked having art directors habitually working all kinds of hours.

The art department is the last stop for an 11th-hour article that needs to run in the magazine.

137

So if I have an editor under my employ who is chronically late with stories, I'll sit him down and try to correct the situation. It's a management point that the art department appreciates.

An ad salesperson's greatest pleasure is closing a magazine with record pages or revenues.

The average salary for an art director who has worked in the business four to 10 years ranges from $41,000 to $43,000. Again, the compensation level is higher if you are working on either the east or west coast, where typically the average salary is around $49,000. An entry-level art director can expect to start anywhere from $22,000 to $28,000, depending on the size of the company.

ADVERTISING SALES

Advertising salespeople are the frontline soldiers on the business side of a magazine. An ad salesperson's greatest pleasure is closing a magazine with record pages or revenues. He delights in converting new sales leads into a steady advertiser.

An ideal advertising salesperson should of course be a sales go-getter, pitching the value of the readership of his magazine. And he should be championing the editorial scope of his magazine. And a really well-trained salesperson can go beyond that. I've trained quite a few advertising salespeople to act as another pair of eyes and ears for their editor. Because salespeople—especially those selling advertising space for business or special-interest magazines—are speaking and meeting with companies who are driving the market, some of the latest-breaking editorial can be cultivated from a salesperson's conversation. This can be hot news, a new product introduction that will revolutionize a market, or a feature that will educate the editor's readership. It's up to the salesperson to recognize what is hot news and what is fluff. Of course this determination comes with experience. But it also comes with having good management overseeing the process.

Accurately forecasting how much you can make selling advertising space in the magazine business is like predicting a weather pattern in January when you're sitting on a beach in July. Why? Because the variables that determine earnings are much more diverse in advertising sales than in any other branch of the business.

First of all, there is the gender gap. Unfortunately, there is a marked difference between male and female advertising salespeople. The male advertising salesperson averages $48,000, while his female colleague earns $36,500. Then, the region of the country you work in, how large your territory is, what your sales volume is in that territory, and whether you work for a small, mid-size or large company will determine your overall compensation package. As a good rule of thumb, your total compensation package should equal approximately 6% to 8% of the revenue you bring to your company.

Be realistic about salary if you are just starting out.

But be realistic if you are just starting out. If you are an entry-level candidate who will be learning on the job, don't expect too much at the beginning. Entry-level salespeople in space sales can expect a base salary from $20,000 (or possibly lower) to $30,000, depending on where you live and the size of the company you work for. Commissions and bonuses might not be offered until six months to a year after you begin

> **The skills needed to be an effective advertising director are vastly different from what it takes to be a star salesperson.**

work. Industry surveys show that business magazines pay more for advertising salespeople than consumer magazines. Why? Since most (but not all) business magazines are mailed free to their readers, the primary revenue stream usually is advertising. Therefore the salesperson has better leverage with his employer, which translates into higher earnings than his consumer counterpart.

The pecking order in advertising sales usually is that after you move up from advertising sales, you become a regional or branch manager. From there you might become an advertising manager or advertising director. A word to the wise: If you become a hot shot advertising salesperson, it doesn't mean you will be successful managing other salespeople. The repertoire of skills needed to be an effective and successful advertising director is vastly different from what it takes to be a star salesperson. Everyone has his own style. And generally, the star salesperson is so fond of his own technique that he has no sensitivity for anyone else's style. This can set the stage for disaster. Sometimes the last person the publisher wants to manage other salespeople is the sales star. The company ends up having its top performer off the front lines, and the superstar ends up alienating the advertising sales staff with an autocratic and boorish style.

As you move up in advertising sales, it would be wise to attend management and motivation courses to learn how to manage a sales staff. If you do reach management status and are successful, your compensation package can run well into the six figures, with all kinds of perks and benefits. Remember, you rise above everyone else through a combination of hard work, luck and a dose of after-hour networking.

CIRCULATION

Recent statistics have revealed a marked increase in salaries for circulation personnel. According to *Folio:*'s surveys, raises for both circulation directors and managers have averaged about 8% over the last several years. The average circulation director in now compensated in the low $50s, while the average salary for a circulation manager is in the mid-$30s. In years past, compensation packages for circulators usually lagged behind everyone, but as magazines have become more aware of the importance of reader and ancillary revenue, salaries have increased.

The circulation director is the person responsible for planning and coordinating the company's circulation marketing efforts. The CD is responsible for single-copy (newsstand) sales, subscription sales, database marketing and list rentals. Salaries for a CD vary widely, depending on variables such as region of the country, the size of the magazine, the number of magazines managed, the number of employees managed and several other factors. Generally, the larger the magazine you manage, the better your compensation package. It's possible for a savvy, top-notch CD who oversees several titles for a large publishing company to earn a compensation package of well into six figures, usually structured as a base salary plus a bonus.

The circulation manager is the person who helps carries out the CD's strategies. The circulation manger administers all the programs for

As magazines have become more aware of the importance of reader and ancillary revenue, salaries have increased.

**Ancillary
revenue
adds to the
publisher's
bottom line.**

either one title or a variety of titles. For the most part, compensation for a circulation manager can vary from the mid-$20s to the mid-$40s. The wide swing is again predicated by the size of the company, etc. An entry-level position averages in the high $20s.

Over the last few years publishing companies have become increasingly more sophisticated through database marketing. Ancillary revenue streams through merchandise such as videos, audio tapes, CD-ROMs, books and a slew of other products have added to the smart publisher's bottom line. Many circulation directors or circulation managers have evolved into the point person for many of these efforts. This additional revenue stream for magazine companies has contributed to the marked increase in circulation salaries.

PRODUCTION

In today's demanding publishing environment, production personnel are being asked to absorb more responsibility than their predecessors. The trend that has expanded the production department's scope is the emergence of today's technology, which has pushed the pre-press aspect of publishing in-house. Moreover, the rise of electronic publishing has joined the production department with the IS department. These influences have increased the production department's workload exponentially. A typical production department today might be asked to traffic and/or produce magazines, books, video packaging, convention newspapers and other projects. A production person may even be asked to double as assistant art director, IS director or web site administrator.

In many publishing companies, there are two levels to the production department: the spot held by the production director, and the secondary position filled by the production manager. The production director, or vice president of manufacturing, is the person who negotiates prices with the printer and other vendors. The production director usually sets the company's publishing schedules and oversees a staff of production managers. At their highest level, production directors average $70,000 per year, depending again on the position's responsibilities. Factors that skewer a production director's compensation are the number of magazines he oversees, employees supervised, circulation of magazines, frequency and total pages published. Several production directors earn a salaries into the six figures, but most of time these salaries are found in very large corporate environments.

Production managers are responsible for overseeing the daily operations of the company. They traffic advertising and, in many instances, editorial material, expedite advertising billing, handle page make-up, check quality control and a multitude of other tasks. For their labors production managers, at their highest levels, average $40,000 to $45,000 a year in salary compensation. This level is usually reached after 10 years on the job. Like the salary of the production director, this average salary can vary depending on the same variables as the production director—number of magazines, frequency, total pages produced and circulation. An entry-level

A production person may be asked to double as assistant art director, IS director or web site administrator.

143

production salary will usually range anywhere
from $19,000 to $27,000 per year.

13

FINDING A JOB IN MAGAZINE PUBLISHING

To find a good job opportunity in magazine publishing, you need time, energy and hard work to open doors. Then you need lots of perseverance, and hope for a dose of good luck. You'll need to plan, prepare and pound the pavement, all with a good measure of enthusiasm and commitment. If you do all these things with all your heart, you'll land a job.

There are many ways to hunt for a job. You should be speaking with personnel agencies. You should be scouring the want ads. You should be reviewing the trade journals that are part of the magazine industry. By far, however, the best way to get yourself hired is through a personal contact in the business. Knowing someone who is working in magazine publishing is your best bet.

Knowing someone who is working in magazine publishing is your best bet.

If you don't know anyone in the magazine business, start the process of making several contacts today. Go to industry conferences that might be taking place in your area. Dedicate some of your time to interning at a publishing company. Write a letter to the publisher of a company you would be interested in, outlining why you want to join his team. Pie in the sky thinking, you say? I don't think so. I've hired people who sent me unsolicited letters. I've hired college interns to full-time positions. And I've met people at magazine conferences looking to break into the business and referred them to my colleagues for a position. The point is, the more visible you become in the industry, the better your chances are of landing a job. Publishers are always looking for good talent.

To best represent you and your experience, of course, you need a professionally written, professionally produced resume and cover letter. Let's talk about the cover letter first.

THE COVER LETTER

The cover letter is essential for your job search, especially if you are a recent college graduate with little or no experience. The cover letter should be tailored to a specific individual in a company. Make certain that you know the correct spelling of the person's name. This detail can cost you a job opportunity. Double check the person's name by asking his secretary. Then double check the spelling again by referring to the masthead of the magazine.

The cover letter gives you the opportunity to outline what specific career opportunity you are searching for. It should be written less formally than your resume, and detail what functions and skills you can offer. Mentioning several ideas that can help the company shows that you're a thinker.

Make the letter brief and to the point. Don't ramble! A brief letter stands a better chance of getting read. Make all your compelling points within the first three paragraphs. Use plain white paper, and type your letter. Before sending out the letter, read it over several times. Then read it again aloud. After you proofread the letter for spelling or grammatical mistakes, have someone else do the same.

> **The cover letter should be tailored to a specific individual.**

Keep in mind the cover letter is the "hook" for the reader to look at your resume. Try to add your personality to your cover letter in some way. A slight tinge of smart humor can work with some people (it works with me!) but not with others. An art director won me over through an intelligent, humorous cover letter. But be careful with humor. Crafted incorrectly, it will turn people off.

When closing your cover letter, don't forget to ask for an interview. That's the main reason you've sent the letter and resume in the first place. Leave off by saying you will be contacting the person soon. This shows your sincere interest in the company.

DESIGNING THE WINNING RESUME

There are hundreds of how-to resume books on the market. Many offer solid advice. But keep in mind the resume will only get you an interview, and not the job. Without question, the best way to get a job is through networking. Talk with family members—even your long-lost Aunt Ethel 3,000 miles away. Friends, friends of friends, people at your place of worship, old college roommates, indeed, everyone you know. Studies show that close to 80% of professionals get their jobs through personal referrals.

If you're not a strong writer—and you should be, especially if you are applying for a publishing position—retain a resume service to help you design an effective resume. Check your phone book for reputable services in your area. Or shop the bookstores or your local library and review the dozens of resume books. There are resume

The best way to get a job is through networking.

Even the most experienced executives with years of professional history limit their resumes to two pages.

templates in these books that will show you how to format your work experience.

Resumes are designed either chronologically, by function, or a combination of both these styles. Review all styles and decide which one you feel more comfortable with. No particular style is the best. The key element to keep in mind is how your prospective employer will read your resume. The resume should be concise and effective in relaying just what talents, skills and abilities you can bring to the company—don't let the reader have to guess what your talents are.

If you don't have any specific skills relevant to the position, stress those skills you think are transferable from your previous work, school or volunteer experience. Often, prospective employers read resumes very quickly—most resumes are never read in their entirety. Tell the reader right off what you can do for him. And tell him how you can do all these wonderful things now, and in the future!

If you are a recent college graduate with little professional experience, don't be shy about relating your experiences from the most mundane jobs. Over the many years that I've interviewed college graduates, I looked favorably on those candidates who have demonstrated a long history of work experience—no matter how mundane or irrelevant. I gauge college graduate applicants on an "ambition index," how committed they are to the work experience. Keep your resume brief. Even the most experienced executives with years of professional history limit their resumes to two pages.

And my final piece of advice is this: Tell the

truth. Don't embellish your resume with skills or talents that you don't have. The conscientious interviewer will find out almost immediately. If you do get past the interview and land a job based on false pretenses, it will soon become apparent that you're a fraud. And you don't want to be known as a fraud in any industry.

THE INTERVIEW

If you are asked to come in for an interview, there are some important things to do prior to meeting with your prospective employer. Most important, and this may sound trite, be prepared to be actually interviewed. This means prepare for some tough, thought-provoking questions by reading up on how to be successfully interviewed. Head to your local library or bookstore for books written on this subject. Regrettably, many people never prepare to be interviewed. They go in to an interview and wing it, and then fail miserably when they do get interviewed by someone who knows how to ask the right questions.

Prepare for some tough, thought-provoking questions.

People I've hired over the years have told me that my interview session was the toughest they've ever had. What's it about my interview that's so different from others? Plain and simple, it's because I ask questions—incisive questions that force candidates to think on their toes. While my interviewing technique is not designed to make anyone uncomfortable, candidates will spend most of the time talking about themselves. With the format of the questions that I ask, I get a good sense of the person's abilities and manageability. But this is not the case for many other

151

interviewers. How often have you gone on an interview where the interviewer spends 90% of the session talking about himself? Or the company? Or he was busy answering the telephone or meeting with people coming in and out of his office? At the end of the session what has he learned about you? Most likely, nothing. Hiring managers like this usually have a high turnover, because they don't properly screen their candidates through an effective interview in the first place. The employee turnover at the companies I've overseen has been very low because I've studied, and continue to study, how to effectively interview, hire and motivate the best hires for my organization. It takes a little extra work on my part, but it pays off in the long run.

When coming in for an interview, know exactly where the company is located. If this means doing a dry run of getting to the company's offices beforehand, do so. You don't want to miscalculate the time it takes you to get to the office on the morning of the interview. Be on time. Come in a few minutes early to get yourself acquainted with the surroundings. But don't have yourself announced until the appointed meeting time. And don't be afraid to ask to use the bathroom. It's better than squirming your way through the interview.

When dressing for an interview, think conservatively. A dark suit for a man or a conservatively styled dress for a woman is always appropriate. Wear little or no cologne or perfume. Make sure your shoes are shined, your hair is neat and clean and your eyeglasses, if you wear them, are clean. When shaking hands with your prospective

> **When dressing for an interview, think conservatively.**

COVER LETTERS, RESUMES AND THE INTERVIEW

employer, look him in the eyes, with as firm a handshake as he gives to you. Do not sit down until you are invited to do so. During the course of the interview, look your interviewer in the eyes, but don't stare. Occasionally, move your eyes to the side. Try to relax. Naturally smile when the situation calls for it. Never force a smile. It always looks phony.

Always tell the truth, no matter how disadvantageous it may seem.

Here's a few more things to watch out for. Don't take off your suit jacket mid-stream, regardless of how warm the office is. Don't lean on the interviewer's desk. Don't lie—always tell the truth, no matter how disadvantageous it may seem to you. Avoid talking politics and religion.

And remember this: If you blow the interview, the sun will still rise tomorrow. So relax and enjoy the experience.

14

ORGANIZATIONS, ASSOCIATIONS, MAGAZINES AND BOOKS IN THE BUSINESS

There are several associations serving the magazine publishing business, on the national, regional or state level. Listed below are the top associations and organizations.

ORGANIZATIONS AND ASSOCIATIONS

American Business Press
875 Third Avenue
New York, NY 10017
Tel: (212) 661-6360
Fax: (212) 370-0736
With a membership of more than 140 trade and consumer magazine companies, the ABP's credo is to actively promote print as a medium of choice to advertisers and advertising agencies.

Several associations serve the magazine publishing business.

Audit Bureau of Circulations
900 North Meacham Road
Schaumburg, IL 60173-4968
Tel: (847) 605-0909
Fax: (847) 605-0483
ABC is a global auditing organization that verifies magazine readership numbers to advertisers, advertising agencies and the media. ABC audits more than 1,400 daily and weekly newspapers, and more than 1,000 periodicals, including paid and non-paid consumer magazines, business publications, farm publications and electronic publications.

155

BPA International
270 Madison Avenue
New York, New York 10016
Tel: (212) 779-3200
Fax: (212) 779-3615
BPA International is a leading international, not-for-profit provider of circulation and interactive marketing intelligence. BPA International has nearly 3,700 members, including 1,700 business magazines and special interest magazines.

Direct Marketing Association
1120 Avenue of the Americas
New York, NY 10036
Tel: (212) 768-7277
Fax: (212) 302-6714
The DMA is an association that serves businesses, including magazine publishers, interested in database marketing. Their Professional Development and Training Department offers a variety of institutes and seminars across the country on a variety of topics.

Fulfillment Management Association Inc.
60 East 42nd Street
New York, NY 10165
Tel: (212) 661-1410
Fax: (212) 277-1597
The Fulfillment Management Association keeps it membership of circulation professionals current on the latest trends and developments in the world of fulfillment and circulation. Membership is open to anyone directly or indirectly involved with serving magazine subscribers.

ORGANIZATIONS, ASSOCIATIONS, MAGAZINES AND BOOKS

Magazine Publishers of America
919 Third Avenue
New York, New York 10022
Tel: (212) 872-3700
Fax: (212) 888-4217
The Magazine Publishers of America is a professional association comprised of nearly 200 magazine companies publishing more than 750 magazines. The MPA's mission is to support and promote the editorial and economic vitality and integrity of MPA member publications. It also strives to be the primary source of information in the publishing industry for its members and at large.

Periodical & Book Association of America, Inc.
475 Park Avenue South, 8th Floor.
New York, NY 10016
Tel: (212) 689-4952
Fax: (212) 545-8328
The PBAA is an association comprised of businesses that deal with periodical and book newsstand sales. It is comprised of publishers, retailers, wholesalers and national distributors from around the country, and holds yearly conferences to discuss industry issues.

Western Publications Association
823 Rim Crest Drive
Westlake Village, CA 91361
Tel: (805) 495-1863
Fax: (805) 497-1849
The Western Publications Associations is an organization serving magazine publishers based west of the Mississippi. It is a very active orga-

157

nization that offers seminars and intern programs for many of its member companies. It
also has a web site—www.wpa-online.org—that
features a job bank. Take a look!

MAGAZINES

Like other industries, the magazine business has
several publications that report on the news and
trends affecting the industry. All are a must-read
for the person seriously considering the magazine publishing business as a career.

Folio:Magazine
11 Riverbend Drive South
PO Box 4949
Stamford, CT 06907-0949
Tel: (203) 358-9900
Fax: (203) 357-9014
Folio: The Magazine for Magazine Management
is written for the magazine publishing team. It
features articles on a variety of magazine management topics, including advertising sales, circulation, editorial, production and electronic
media. It's a great magazine for the budding
professional.

Circulation Management Magazine
11 Riverbend Drive South
PO Box 4235
Stamford, CT 06907-0235
Tel: (203) 358-9900
Fax: (203) 358-5823
Highly respected in the publishing industry,
Circulation Management is edited for circula-

tion directors and managers, publishers, and other circulation professionals in the magazine publishing industry. Topics covered include subscription renewals, direct mail, products, literature, services and postal updates. If your interests lie in magazine circulation, this magazine is for you.

MagazineRetailer
124 West 24th Street
New York, NY 10011
Tel: (212) 989-6978
Fax: (212) 255-7143
MagazineRetailer is for the magazine professional interested in single copy or newsstand sales. The magazine offers a variety of information, including trends in the newsstand business, new magazine introductions, profiles of innovative retailers who sell magazines, directory listings, new launches and other pertinent information.

Publishing and Production Executive
401 N. Broad Street
Philadelphia, PA 19108
Tel: (215) 238-5300
Fax: (215) 238-5457
Publishing and Production Executive is targeted at magazine production managers. It includes case studies on production people and their magazines, as well as new products, services and management tips. It's a great resource for staying up on the ongoing trends in the magazine publishing industry as they relate to print production.

159

Advertising Age
220 East 42nd Street
New York, NY 10017-5846
Tel: (212) 210-0171
Fax: (212) 210-0200
Advertising Age reports on the advertising
industry as well as magazine publishing. Their
editorial is geared more toward company and
personnel news than to how-to pieces. Ad Age,
as everyone in the industry calls it, is a must-
read for what's happening in the industry.

AdWeek
1515 Broadway
New York, NY 10036
Tel: (212) 536-5336
Fax: (212) 536-5353
AdWeek is a weekly news magazine edited pri-
marily for advertising agency professionals,
although magazine publishing news is covered
too. The magazine provides local and national
news, people profiles, and other topics germane
to advertising and magazine publishing.

Digital Production Executive
11 Riverbend Drive South
PO Box 4949
Stamford, CT 06907-0949
Tel: (203) 358-9900
Fax: (203) 357-9014
Digital Production Executive focuses on pre-
press technology and production management.
It is an in-depth, state-of-the-art magazine for
experienced magazine production managers

who select and supervise pre-publishing and digital processes. It's definitely worth a look if your interest is in publication production.

Additional magazine titles that may be of interest include *Magazine & Bookseller* (215) 238-5300; *Catalog Age* and *Direct Magazine*, both can be reached at (203) 358-9900; *Direct Marketing Magazine* (516) 746-6700; *DM News* (212) 741-2095; and *Target Marketing Magazine* (215) 238-5300.

RESOURCES

To get a really big picture of the magazine business, there are several resource directories and databases of magazines—broken down by consumer and business-to-business titles. These resources will generally offer a brief synopsis of the editorial scope of the magazine as well as contact names, addresses, telephone numbers and faxes.

Oxbridge Communications
150 Fifth Avenue
New York, NY 10011
Tel: (800) 955-0231
Fax: (212) 633-2938
Oxbridge has one of the largest databases of magazines and catalogs. And the nice thing about their database is that it's available on their web site (www.mediafinder.com).
Oxbridge publishes a variety of comprehensive directories and databases, including their National Directory of Magazines, available at

161

most libraries.
SRDS
1700 Higgins Road
Des Plaines, Illinois 60018-5605
Tel: (800) 851-7737
For nearly 80 years, SRDS has provided the advertising and media industry with comprehensive listings of the media business. Although these directories are designed for the media buyer planning an advertising campaign, they are very useful as a resource guide for the career planner. SRDS publishes two distinct volumes for the magazine industry. The yellow volume encapsulates the consumer magazine market. The green volume is the business-to-business directory.

PubList.com
800 Hingham Street
Rockland, MA 02370
Tel: (781) 792-0999
PubList.com (www.publist.com) databases more than 140,000 active publications on its web site. Its on-line database is searchable by publication name.

15

COLLEGES, EXTENSION PROGRAMS, PROFESSIONAL SEMINARS AND SUMMER INSTITUTES

There are many fine publishing programs around the country offering syllabuses designed for a career in magazine publishing. Here is a listing of such programs. Some are offered as undergraduate and graduate courses, and some are offered as college extension, adult education certificate courses or summer institutes.

CREDIT AND CERTIFICATE PROGRAMS

Many fine publishing programs offer syllabuses designed for a career in magazine publishing.

New York University Center for Publishing
48 Cooper Square
Room 101
New York, NY 10003
Tel: (212) 998-9123
New York University offers three publishing programs. The school's for-credit program is a Masters in Science in Publishing, which offers a concentration in magazine publishing. There are two other programs. One is NYU's Certificate in Magazine Publishing program, which is part of the University's Adult Education School. The other program is a three-week intensive course, usually held in the summer.

Pace University
Midtown Center
535 Fifth Avenue, 4th Floor
New York, NY 10016
Tel: (800) 874-PACE

165

Pace University's M.S. in Publishing prepares students for book, magazine or electronic publishing. Its core curriculum offers courses in Magazine Production and Design, Financial Aspects of Publishing and Editorial Principles and Practices. Using elective courses such as Magazine Advertising Sales or Magazine Circulation, students can create a concentration in a specialized area of interest. A student can take up to four classes in the curriculum as a non-matriculating student.

George T. Dellacorte Magazine Program
The Columbia Graduate School of Journalism
2960 Broadway
New York, NY 10027
Tel: (212) 854-3828
Columbia's magazine program is a concentration of its M.S. in Journalism degree. While there are several courses that analyze the business of the magazine industry, the syllabus is focused more heavily on editing and writing. Encompassing two semesters, the program features workshops and guest speakers.

Radcliffe College Publishing Course
77 Brattle Street
Cambridge, MA 02138
Tel: (617) 495-8678
For more than 50 years Radcliffe Publishing Course has provided an intensive introduction to all facets of book and magazine publishing. Instructors and lecturers are drawn from all sections of the publishing industry. Small workshops are held throughout the course to teach various publishing fundamentals.

Stanford
Box SF
Stanford Professional Publishing
Stanford, CA 94305-4005
Tel: (650) 725-6259
www.stanfordproed.org
An intensive 13-day course on magazine and book publishing, this program is geared more to magazine professionals already in the business. Presented by leaders in the publishing industry, Stanford's course includes seminars and case studies in editing, production, design, marketing, circulation, sales, advertising, finance, new technology and publishing law.

Felker Magazine Center
Graduate School of Journalism
North Gate Hall
University of California
Berkeley, CA 94720
Tel: (510) 642-3383
Clay Felker, Director: (510) 643-8254
The center offers a sequence of four magazine publishing courses integrated into the journalism school curriculum, and lectures and conferences presented by experts in publishing.

Medill School of Journalism
Magazine Publishing Project
Northwestern University
1845 Sheridan Road
Evanston, IL 60208
Tel: (847) 467-4159
Under the guidance of instructors, graduate study magazine students research and select an

original, publishable idea and assign staff positions, including publisher, editors, artists, market researchers, advertising salespeople, a circulation team and a business manager. Since the program began in 1981, 29 original consumer and trade magazines have been produced in the class; many have won national awards.

University of Missouri School of Journalism
213A Walter Williams Hall
Columbia, MO 65211
Tel: (573) 882-4821
The magazine sequence of Missouri's School of Journalism prepares students for careers as writers, editors and designers. The sequence consists of 33 hours within the School of Journalism. Course work is flexible and depends on career interest. Electives include Magazine Production, Advanced Magazine Design and Magazine Editing.

SEMINARS AND INTERNSHIPS

The Folio: Show
11 River Bend Drive South
Box 4232
Stamford, CT 06907-0232
Tel: (203) 358-3751
Sponsored by *Folio:Magazine*, the magazine that writes and reports on the magazine business, Folio: Shows offers a full slate of seminars presented by industry professionals. With a seminar track that numbers more than a dozen categories, and with each category offering an average of 10 seminars, these shows offer the neo-

phyte (and the not-so-neophyte) publishing professional a wide range of topics germane to magazine publishing. Folio: Shows are held through the year in New York, Chicago and Los Angeles. These are "must-attend" seminars for the new publishing professional.

Circulation Management Conference & Expo
11 River Bend Drive South
Box 4232
Stamford, CT 06907-0232
Tel: (203) 358-3751
If magazine circulation is your game, then you'll want to check out this conference and expo. Held in June in New York City by *Circulation Management Magazine*, the conference presents every imaginable topic related to magazine circulation. It consists of 30 in-depth seminars conducted by circulation professionals for circulation professionals.

Magazine Publishers of America
919 Third Avenue
New York, NY 10022
Tel: (212) 872-3700
The MPA offers nearly 100 practical seminars and workshops on all disciplines of magazine publishing through its Professional Development program. It recently began a comprehensive, three-day training program for beginning professionals. Conducted by industry experts, the programs are open to members of MPA as well as non-members (usually there is a slight surcharge for non-members.) Call the MPA for a seminar schedule.

169

American Society of Magazine Editors
919 Third Avenue
New York, NY 10022
Tel: (212) 872-3700
The ASME offers a ten-week summer editorial intern program for college juniors who are majoring in journalism or college students who are heavily involved in campus publishing.

16

PERSONNEL AGENCIES SERVICING THE MAGAZINE PUBLISHING BUSINESS

The following personnel agencies are active in magazine publishing. The bold listings represent those companies who will place entry level candidates or candidates with minimal experience. The other listed companies strictly place individuals in either middle or senior level positions. Call each company to determine area of specialty.

Ariel Associates
410 West 53d Street, Suite 126
New York, NY 10019
Contact: Gene Fixler
Tel: (212) 765-8300
Fax: (212) 765-3450

Berardi and Associates
1140 Avenue of the Americas, 9th Floor
New York, NY 10036
Contact: Loretta Berardi
Tel: (212) 382-1616
Fax: (212) 764-9690

Berkana International, Inc.
3417 Fremont Avenue North, Suite 225
Seattle, WA 98103
Contact: Sonia Carson
Tel: (206) 547-3226
Fax: (206) 547-3843
Electronic Publishing

Bert Davis
425 Madison Avenue
New York, NY 10017
Contact: Wendy Baker
Tel: (212) 8384000
Fax: (212) 935-3291

Career Blazers
590 Fifth Avenue
New York, NY 10036
Contact: Michele Horri
Tel: (212) 719-3232
Fax: (212) 921-1827

Carlsen Resources
800 Belford Avenue Suite 200
Grand Junction, CO 81501
Contact: Ann Carlsen
Tel: (970) 242-9462
Fax: (970) 242-9074

Crandall Associates, Inc.
114 East 32nd Street, Suite 1202
New York, NY 10016
Contact: Hal Crandall
Tel: (212) 213-1700
Fax: (212) 696-1287

Eden Personnel, Inc.
280 Madison Avenue
New York, NY 10016
Contact: Kevin Cogan
Tel: (212) 685-8600
Fax: (212) 779-9579

Executive Search Partners
444 Park Avenue South
New York, NY 10016
Contact: Kenneth Collins
Tel: (212) 686-2929
Fax: (212) 686-2172

Farrell & Phin
845 Third Avenue
New York, NY 10022
Contact: Frank Farrell or Jane Phin
Tel: (212) 838-5511
Fax: (212) 593-0378

Gardner Associates, Inc.
300 Madison Avenue,
16th Floor
New York, NY 10017
Contact: Elsa Ross
Tel: (212) 687-6615
Fax: (212) 697-9135

Graphic Arts Marketing Associates
3533 Deepwood Drive
Lambertville, MI 48144
Fax: (313) 854-5224
Graphic arts personnel specialists

Heidrick & Struggles, Inc.
245 Park Avenue, Suite 4300
New York, NY 10167
Contact: Orlin Davis
Tel: (212) 867-9876
Fax: (212) 370-9035

Helen Akullian
280 Madison Avenue
New York, NY 10016
Contact: Helen Akullian
Tel: (212) 532-3210
Fax: (212) 889-8631

Howard-Sloan-Koller Group
353 Lexington Avenue
New York, NY 10016
Contact: Ed Koller
Tel: (212) 661-5250
Fax: (212) 557-9178

Jesse Reid Associates
152-½ East 63th Street
New York, NY 10021
Contact: Georgia Petry
Tel: (212) 355-1300
Fax: (212) 355-1648

Kresin Wingard
333 N. Michigan Avenue, Suite 622
Chicago, IL 60601
Contact: David Wingard
Tel: (312) 726-8676
Fax: (312) 726-4705

Korn/Ferry International
200 Park Avenue, 11th Floor
New York, NY 10021
Contact: Mary Summers
Tel: (212) 687-1834
Fax: (212) 986-5684

Lamay Associates, Inc.
P0 Box 517
Riverside, CT 06878
Contact: Lawrence Mayers
Tel: (914) 764-4020
Fax: (914) 764-4054

Milo Research
305 Madison Avenue, Suite 1762
New York, NY 10017
Contact: Lance Goulbourne
Tel: (212) 972-2780
Fax: (212) 983-5854

Nordeman Grimm, Inc.
717 Fifth Avenue, 26th Floor
New York, NY 10022
Contact: David Bentley
Tel: (212) 935-1000
Fax: (212) 980-1443

Ribolow Associates
230 Park Avenue
New York, NY 10169
Contact: Adele Ribolow
Tel: (212) 808-0580
Fax: (212) 573-6050

Ridenour & Associates
1 East Wacker Drive
Chicago, IL 60601
Contact: Suzanne Ridenour
Tel: (312) 644-1888
Fax: (312) 644-1883

Russell Reynolds Associates
200 Park Avenue, 23rd Floor
New York, NY 10166
Contact: Hobson Brown, Jr.
Tel: (212) 351-2000
Fax: (212) 370-0896

Sally Reich Associates
50 Sutton Place South
New York, NY 10166
Contact: Sally Reich
Tel: (212) 308-3276
Fax: (212) 308-9453

The Lynne Palmer Agency
342 Madison Avenue, Suite 1430
New York, NY 10173
Contact: Sara Nolfo
Tel: (212) 883-0203
Fax: (212) 883-0149

The Sales Athlete
8844 West Olympic Blvd.
Beverly Hills, CA 90211
Contact: Nancy Leeds
Tel: (310) 275-8900
Fax: (310) 248-2441

Walker Communications
1212 Avenue of the Americas
New York, NY 10036
Contact: Martin Walker, Shanna Silver
Tel: (212) 944-0011
Fax: (212) 944-2263

Ward Howell International
99 Park Avenue
New York, NY 10016
Contact: Carrie Pryor
Tel: (212) 697-3730
Fax: (212) 697-1398

Zachary & Sanders, Inc.
82 North Broadway
Hicksville, NY 11801
Contact: Richard Zachary
Tel: (516) 922-5500
Fax: (516) 922-2286

For further research check out a valuable resource called *The Directory of Executive Recruiters*, published by Kennedy Publications. The recruiters listed are indexed by industry, function and geography. While many of the recruiters listed serve senior-level executives, there is quite a number of listings for less-experienced candidates. Check your local library or bookstore.

17

A BASIC MAGAZINE
OPERATING STATEMENT

If you decide to start your own magazine, here is a sample magazine operating statement.

INCOME
Advertising—Net of agency commissions and
                       cash discounts
New subscriptions
Renewal subscriptions
Single copy sales
Ancillary income

EXPENSES
Manufacturing
    Paper
    Printing
    Postage
    Single copy distribution
    Production department
Advertising
    Salaries and commissions
    Travel and entertainment
    Support salaries
    Branch office costs
    Promotion and research
    Other
Editorial
    Salaries
    Contributors
    Artwork, photos
    Travel and entertainment

Subscriptions
  Salaries
  New subscription promotions
  Renewal subscription promotions
  Fulfillment
  Other
Single Copy
  Salaries
  Travel and entertainment
  Promotion
  Freight
General and Administrative
  Salaries
  Travel and entertainment
  Occupancy
  Payroll taxes
  Professional services
  Taxes (other than income)
  Office costs
  Other

18

GLOSSARY OF MAGAZINE TERMS

While not intended to be definitive, the following is a list of basic terms found in magazine publishing that should be helpful to those new to the magazine publishing business.

CIRCULATION TERMS

ABC (Audit Bureau of Circulations): ABC currently has 4,556 members, including 803 consumer titles, 315 business and farm publications, and 1,367 newspapers. ABC audits members' readerships so that advertisers and ad agencies know how many readers they are buying when they advertise in a publication.

Advertiser Copies: Each advertiser in a given issue is commonly sent a copy of the issue so that the advertiser can check the ad. Also called a comp copy.

Agent-Sold Subs: Paid subscriptions sold by commissionable outside agencies, as opposed to subs promoted by the magazine publisher.

Alternate Source: Any subscription promotion source other than direct mail. They can encompass TV, radio, telemarketing, and a variety of other avenues of subscription promotion.

Audit Bureau: Organizations that audit the claimed circulations of their publisher members for purposes of substantiating those claims for advertisers. ABC and BPA International are the most significant audit bureaus.

Automatic Renewal: When a subscriber agrees to allow a magazine publisher to continue to renew the subscription using the subscriber's initial credit card authorization.

Back Copies: Copies served to a new subscriber that are older than the current issue. Often used to help meet paid rate base or controlled circulation goals.

Bad Pay: Subscriptions the publisher suspends for nonpayment.

Basic Rate: A magazine's standard, published subscription price, usually for one year.

Bind-in Card: A return postcard inserted by the publisher into a magazine for subscription promotion. Or an advertiser promotion.

Blow-in Card: A subscription promotion card not bound into the magazine. A traditional source for magazine publishers to generate subscriptions.

Bulk Subscriptions: Multiple subscriptions sold to one customer, usually at a discount.

Catalog Agency: A company other than the magazine publisher that sells subscriptions.

CD: Acronym for Circulation Director.

Circulation: A magazine's total net paid subscriptions and single copies and/or request and qualified recipients.

Consumer Marketing Director: A title for circulation directors that has evolved due to the trend to develop new consumer products.

Control: The basic mailing package against whose results other direct mail subscription promotion packages are compared. Usually, the control is the winning package from a previous mailing.

Controlled Circulation: Many business/trade publications, and some consumer publications, are sent free of charge to individuals who qualify because they work within a certain industry, have a certain job title, purchase certain types of products, or otherwise represent a targeted group of particular interest to specific types of advertisers.

Conversion: A first-time renewal, or converting non-paid subscribers to paid subscribers.

Database Marketing: Database marketing allows magazine publishers to cross-sell or upsell products to its subscribers based on a subscriber's profile. Within a subscriber's profile are variables that can include a subscriber's past purchase history, zip code, main interest and many other variables.

Demographics: The characteristics of a magazine's readership, including age, gender, household income, schooling, job description and a host of other data.

Donor: A purchaser of a gift subscription.

Double Postcard: A popular subscription promotion mailer that features the magazine's offer and a perforated return postcard.

DRTV (Direct Response Television): A subscription promotion source used by some consumer (and in some instances) business magazines.

Effort: A subscription promotion—usually as part of a series—to an existing or potential subscriber, to either generate new business, renew existing business or qualify (or re-qualify) a controlled reader.

Expire(s): When a subscription lapses without

renewing. Or a list of subs that will expire with a given issue. Or a list of expired subscribers.

Forced Free Trial: A short-term, free subscription sent without request to targeted prospects with the goal of converting them to paid subscribers. This strategy is more common for newsletter publishers.

Freemium: A gift mailed free to a potential subscriber to motivate the prospect to subscribe.

Frequency: The number of times per year that a magazine is published.

Fulfillment: A comprehensive term describing the variety of tasks involved in creating, updating and maintaining an active subscriber list. Magazine publishers either retain a fulfillment house or service bureau, or fulfill their magazines internally with their own staff.

Grace Copies: Copies served to subscribers after expiration. Usually, but not always, magazine publishers will serve one or two grace copies per expire.

Gross Response: The number of initial orders received generated by a subscription promotion effort. Calculated as a percentage of the total pieces mailed.

Hard Offer: When the prospective reader must pay the invoice first before receiving his first issue.

Installment Billing: A subscription offer that allows a subscriber to pay in installments. Most payments are due by the first three or four months of the subscription.

Issue: The date that appears on the cover of the magazine. Usually not the on-sale date of the issue.

List Broker: A company that acts as a liaison between a list renter and a list owner.

List Manager: Either an in-house staff person or a vendor responsible for maintaining and marketing a subscriber list.

Mainfile: The master computer file of a magazine's subscriber list, usually maintained on tape or a disk. Contains name, address and other information, such as price and term, expire issue, start issue, payment status and sales method. B-to-B magazines' masterfiles usually contain detailed demographics.

Merge/Purge: To combine two or more lists by computer, to weed out duplicate names so that the prospective subscribers will not receive duplicate copies of the same promotion.

Model: A circulation model is used to forecast overall financials and circulation levels or revenue. Usually done through software utilizing spreadsheet programs, although some magazine publishers model manually.

Psychographics: Research that profiles a subscriber's lifestyle.

Publisher's Statement: Filed by a publisher twice per year with an audit bureau, a publisher's statement details a magazine's circulation.

Qualified Subscriber/Recipient: A subscriber who meets the reader requirements of a publication. Controlled readers are also known as recipients.

Rate Base: Many publishers guarantee advertisers that they will maintain a certain average circulation level, or rate base, over time. Advertisers use the ratebase to calculate their cost per thousand of circulation, or CPM.

Remit: The revenue paid to a publisher after a subscription agent's commission is deducted.

Renewal Series: A series of direct mail efforts sent to a group of subscribers. Usually starts well before expiration date and generally continues a few months past expiration date.

Self-Mailer: Promotion mail that is not enclosed in an envelope and is designed so that a portion of it can be used for a reply. A double postcard is an example of a self-mailer.

Soft Offer: A subscription offer that gives the prospect options. The subscriber is not obligated to send money to begin receiving the subscription—and before he sends money—he can cancel the subscription after receiving his first "free" issue.

Source: The channel of sale that generated the subscription.

Stampsheet Agencies: Companies that use cooperative direct mail packages to sell subs for a variety of magazines. The two most popular are Publishing Clearing House and American Family Publishers.

Telemarketing: Selling subscriptions by telephone, or by getting the prospect to respond by phone to a DRTV or other subscription promotion.

White Mail: Unsolicited subscription orders or letters.

NEWSSTAND TERMS

Allotment: The allotment is the number of copies of a title shipped to the wholesaler or retailer. It is also known as the draw or allocation. Most times, allotment is used to describe the number of copies shipped to a wholesaler, and draw refers to the copies shipped to a retailer.

Arrival Date: The date of the magazine's actual arrival at the wholesaler.

Authorization: In newsstand sales, a retailer's approval for a particular title to be carried in some or all of its stores (see chain authorization).

Authorized Chains: List of chains that have authorized a title for distribution into their stores.

Bipad: A five-digit code assigned by national newsstand distributors for all magazines. Wholesalers use the bipad to determine which national distributor is supplying a specific magazine to them, as well as to set up distribution, billing and credit systems.

Break-up Agent: A regional trucking company that often receives magazines directly from the printing plant and distributes the magazines to various cities in their geographic area. This shipping company, which handles this breakdown of individual shipments, is also known as a reforwarder or reforwarding agent.

Brokerage: The commission a national distributor takes on copies sold off the newsstand.

Chain Authorization: To get distribution in a chain's stores for a new or existing title, a sales call must be made to the chain buyer to get approval to place a title on the chain's authorized list.

Checkout Racks: Retail display fixtures that are placed at the checkout (cash register) of retail outlets. These fixtures generate higher unit sales than a mainline account, and are usually purchased by large, advertising-based titles. The cost includes the actual cost of the rack and generally a quarterly fixed payment.

Comparative Title: When completing a distribution, a newsstand director uses as few as one or as many as five comparative titles to identify which retailers have the potential to sell a magazine similar in editorial content. A demographic category (men, women, children, etc.) may be used if there are no competitive titles published or approved for distribution.

Direct Accounts: Any retailer who receives their magazines directly from the publisher or through a distributor, bypassing the wholesaler system.

Discount: The wholesaler's price on a given title.

Display: The way a magazine is displayed at a retailer. A full cover display at any retail outlet is best.

Draw: The total number of copies a retailer or wholesaler receives for sale.

Mainline: Generally referred to as a reading center in most supermarkets. It is a large magazine rack displayed within the interior store aisles. In some stores a mainline can be a wall fixture, while in others it can be a free-standing rack in the middle of a store aisle.

National Distributor: A company that is responsible for the distribution, billing and sales and marketing of magazine titles on a national level.

One-Shot: A special edition of a regularly published magazine, or a special issue of a magazine that usually has no more than an annual frequency.

Pick n Pack: When magazine orders are prepared at a central location and then sent via common carrier or shipper directly to retail accounts. This process is generally handled by a direct-to-retail supplier other than the traditional wholesaler.

Polybag: When a magazine is delivered to the newsstand or to the subscriber with a plastic wrap surrounding it. Used to package advertising, editorial or circulation supplements.

Premature Returns: These are returns of a given issue returned by retailers to wholesalers and then to the publisher before the off-sale date.

Promotion: A marketing program designed to increase consumer awareness and sales of an established, new or upcoming title. Retail promotions can be in the form of giveaways and sweepstakes, and generally include ancillary displays.

RDA (or Retail Display Agreement): An agreed-upon percentage of the cover price paid by the publisher to the retailer after the issue of a given title is closed. Retailers typically submit claims through an authorized third party (an RDA consultant), who then submits a claim to the national distributor for payment on behalf of the publisher.

Redistribution: A new distribution made for an on-sale issue for the purpose of maximizing sales during the on-sale period.

Returns: Copies of an issue returned by retail-

193

ers and wholesalers for credit at the end of the sales period.

Sales Date: The date an issue is scheduled to go on-sale. Generally (but not always) magazines go on-sale on Tuesdays or Thursdays.

Single-Copy Sales: Issues sold through a retail environment. Also known as newsstand sales.

UPC (Universal Product Code): The system used for identifying magazines sold in retail outlets. The UPC consists of a manufacturer's code and bipad, and usually appears on the magazine's front cover.

Withholding: When a wholesaler doesn't invoice and deliver all or a portion of his original allotment prescribed by the magazine publisher and the national distributor.

Wholesaler: A company that distributes magazines and books on an ongoing basis to retail accounts in a given region.

PRODUCTION AND EDITORIAL TERMS

AA (Author's Alteration): A text change made on a proof.

Advance: Money paid to an author prior to publication.

Absorption: The property of paper that causes it to absorb ink.

Accordion Fold: In binding, a term used for two or more parallel folds that open like an accordion.

Basis Weight: The weight in pounds of a ream (500 sheets) of paper cut to a given standard size for that grade.

Bit: In computers, the basic unit of digital

information; contraction of BInary digiT.

Black: One of the four colors used in process color printing.

Black-and-White: Originals or reproductions in single color, as distinguished from multicolor.

Bleed: An extra amount of printed image that extends beyond the trim edge of the sheet or page.

Blowup: A photographic enlargement.

Blueline: A pre-press proof that shows the pages either blue on white or blue on yellow.

Body Type: The type used for the main part or text of a printed piece, as distinguished from the heading.

Boldface Type: A name given to type that is darker than the text type with which it is used.

Brightness: The reflectance or brilliance of the paper.

Bulk: The degree of thickness of paper.

Byte: In computers, a unit of digital information, equivalent to one character or eight to 32 bits.

Camera Ready: Copy that is ready for photography.

Caption: Text accompanying a photo or illustration.

CD-ROM: Acronym for Compact Disc-Read-Only Memory. A CD-ROM drive uses the CD format as a computer storage medium.

Character: A single typed letter or symbol.

CMYK: Cyan, magenta, yellow, black—printing colors for process color reproduction. Also called 4-color process.

Coated Paper: Paper having a surface coating that produces a smooth finish. Surfaces vary

195

from eggshell to glossy.

Color Balance: The correct combination of cyan, magenta and yellow to reproduce a photograph without a color cast, produce a neutral gray, or reproduce the colors in the original scene or object.

Color Correction: Any method used to improve color rendition, such as masking, dot-etching, re-etching and scanning.

Color Separation: The process of separating color originals into the primary printing color components in negative or positive form.

Condensed Type: A narrow or slender typeface.

Contrast: The tonal gradation between the highlights, middle tones and shadows in an original or reproduction.

Copy: Furnished manuscript material.

Copyright: The right to retain or sell copies of artistic works.

Croms: Off-press color proofs made using Dupont cromalin materials.

Crop: To eliminate portions of the copy, usually on a photograph or plate, indicated on the original by crop marks.

CTP (Computer-to-Plate): An electronic process in which the printing plate is made directly from a digital file, thus eliminating film.

Cyan: A greenish blue. One of the four colors used in process color printing.

Density: The degree of darkness of a photographic image.

Digital Color Proof: An off-press color proof produced from digital data without the need for separation films.

Dot: The individual element of a halftone.

Dot Gain: In printing, a defect in which dots print larger than they should, causing darker tones or stronger colors.

Dots Per Inch (DPI): A measure of the resolution of a screen image or printed page.

Drop Out: Portions of originals that do not reproduce, especially colored lines or background areas (often on purpose). Also called knockout.

Dummy: A preliminary layout showing the position of illustrations and text as they are to appear in the final reproduction. A set of blank pages made up in advance to show the size, shape, form and general style of a piece of printing.

Duotone: Term for a two-color halftone reproduction from a one-color photograph.

Duplicating: The process of making additional film from an original piece of film. Also called duping.

Emulsion Side: The side of the film coated with the silver halide emulsion.

Em Dash: A dash the width of an "M."

En Dash: A dash the width of an "N."

End Slug: A distinctive symbol signifying the end of a story or article.

Fifth Color: An additional color beyond the capabilities of the four-color process. Examples include metallic and dayglo colors.

Flat: Stripped pages that will all print on the same side of a sheet of paper.

Flatbed Scanner: A device that scans images in a manner similar to a photocopy machine; the original art is placed face down on a glass plate.

Flop: To flip over a photograph so that the image is reversed.

Folio: The page number of a magazine.

Font: A complete assortment of letters, numbers, punctuation marks, etc. of a given type size and design.

Footline: Text on the bottom of the page that shows month, year and name of title.

Form: In offset printing, the assembly of pages and other images for printing.

Four Color Process: Reproduction of full-color art or photographs through the use of several plates (usually four), each printing a different color.

Galley: Proof of text copy before it is made into pages.

Gutter: The blank space or inner margin from the printing area to the binding.

Halftone: The reproduction of artwork such as a photograph, through a contact screen, which converts the image into dots of various sizes.

Hard Copy: Typescript or printed copy, as opposed to copy stored on magnetic tape, disk, etc.

Hickeys: Imperfections in the printing process due to dirt or dust on the printing press.

Highlight: The lightest or whitest parts in a photograph, represented in a halftone reproduction by the smallest dots or the absence of dots.

Hue: The main attribute of a color that distinguishes it from other colors.

Imagesetter: In computer imaging, a device that outputs type, line art and photos in position onto film.

Imposition: The arranging of pages in a press

form to ensure the correct order after the printed sheet is folded and trimmed.

Ink Fountain: The device that stores and supplies ink to the inking rollers on a printing
press.

Insert: A printed piece prepared for insertion
into a publication.

Justify: To set type in lines of equal length,
resulting in an even right-hand margin.

Kerning: The distance between characters in a
word.

Kill Fee: A fee paid to a writer whose assigned
story is not published.

Lamination: A plastic film bonded by heat and
pressure to a printed sheet for protection or
appearance.

Layout: The drawing or sketch of a proposed
printed piece.

Leading: The vertical distance between lines of
type measured in points.

Line Art: A black and white illustration that
does not need screening.

Local Area Network (LAN): The linking of
workstations, storage units (file servers) and
printing devices (print servers).

Logo: The name of a company or product
in a special design used as a trademark in
advertising.

Lowercase: The small letters in type, as
opposed to capital letters.

M: Abbreviation for a quantity of 1000 sheets
of paper.

Machine Coated: Paper that is coated on one
or two sides on a paper machine.

Magenta: A bluish red, one of the four process

199

colors used in process color printing.

Magnetic Storage: Any disk, film, drum or core used to store digital information.

Makeready: All work done to set up a press for printing.

Margin: The white space around the copy on a page.

Matte Finish: Dull paper finish without gloss or luster.

Mechanical: A term for a camera-ready paste-up of artwork. It includes type, photos, line art, etc., all on a piece of artboard.

Moiré: An undesirable screen pattern caused by incorrect screen angles of overprinting halftones.

Montage: A photograph in which several images are combined.

Mottle: The spotty or uneven appearance of printing, mostly in solid areas.

OCR (Optical Character Recognition): Software that allows a computer to read printed or written information—and then digitize it.

Opacity: The property of paper that minimizes the show-through of printing from the back side or the next sheet.

Opaque: The property that makes paper less transparent.

Overlay: A transparent covering over artwork or copy showing color break, instructions or corrections.

Overrun: Copies printed in excess of the specified quantity.

Packager: A person who provides editorial services to a magazine publisher in developing a magazine or a specific issue.

Page Makeup: Assembling all the elements to make up a page.

Pagination: The numbering of pages in a magazine. Also, a graphical representation of all of the pages of a given issue of a magazine. Other terms used are "blueprint" or "flowsheet."

Palette: The collection of colors or shades available to a graphic system or program.

Pantone Matching System: A standardized system for matching colors from PMS swatch books to the ink formulas required on press.

Perfect Binding: When a magazine is bound using glue rather than staples. Perfect binding results in a square spine.

Pica: Printer's unit of measurement used principally in typesetting. One pica equals approximately $\frac{1}{6}$ of an inch.

Pixel: In electronic imaging, a basic unit of digital imaging.

Point: Printer's unit of measurement used for sizing typefaces. There are 72 points to an inch.

Positive: Film containing an image in which the dark and light values are the same as the original. The reverse of negative.

Press Proofs: In color reproduction, a proof of a color subject made on a printing press, in advance of the production run.

Press Run: The number of magazine copies printed. Also called print run.

Process Colors: Yellow, magenta and cyan, plus black in four-color process printing.

Progressive Proofs (Progs): Proofs made from the separate plates in color process work, showing the sequence of printing and the result after each additional color has been applied.

Public Domain: Published material not protected by copyright.

Ream: Five hundred sheets of paper.

Register: Conforming two or more printing images in exact alignment with each other.

Register Marks: Crosses or other targets applied to original copy prior to photography. Used for positioning films in register, or for register of two or more colors.

Resolution: The printout quality using the number of dots per inch.

Reverse: To print an image white on black, rather than black on white. Also called neg.

RGB: The additive primary colors of Red, Green and Blue. The colors by which all computer screens are composed.

Right-Reading: A photographic image in which the right-to left orientation appears as in the original subject; wrong-reading would be the opposite, or a mirror image.

Rosette Pattern: The dot pattern desired when 4-color printing is done correctly. Opposite of moiré, which is an unwanted visual effect produced when screen angles are not controlled during multi-color printing.

Runaround: When text is set around a photo or illustration.

Running Head: A headline or title repeated at the top of each page.

Saddle Wire: To fasten a magazine by wiring it with staples through the middle fold of the sheets.

Serif: The short cross-lines at the ends of the main strokes of letters in some type faces. Sans serif type does not have these lines.

Signature: The name given to a printed sheet after it has been folded.

Silhouette Halftone: A halftone with all of the background removed.

Skid: A platform support for a pile of cut sheets of paper.

Spec: When a freelance writer submits an unsolicited manuscript.

Spot Color: The addition of one PMS color to black in a printed piece.

Stet: A proofreader's mark, written in the margin, signifying that copy marked for corrections should remain as it was.

Stock: Paper or other material to be printed.

Stripping: The positioning of negatives (or positives) on a flat to compose a page or layout for platemaking.

SWOP: Acronym for the term Specifications for Web Offset Publications.

Tabloid: Format used mainly by newspapers but also by many trade magazines. In the magazine business, a tabloid is an oversize magazine.

Text: The body matter of a page or book, as distinguished from the headings.

Transpose: In proofreading or editing, switching the positions of two words, sentences, paragraphs, etc.

Trim Marks: Marks placed on the copy to indicate the edge of the page.

Unjustified Type: A ragged right-hand margin resulting from type set in lines of unequal length.

Varnish: The application of a clear, shiny coating to a printed piece. Usually added for protection and appearance.

Web: A roll of paper used in web or rotary printing.
Web Press: A press which prints on roll- or web-fed paper.
Widow: In composition, a single word on a line by itself that ends a paragraph, or a single word that starts a page.
Work for Hire: Work for which the writer or artist does not retain ownership of the material created.

ADVERTISING SALES TERMS

Advertiser's Copy: An issue sent free to an advertiser by the publisher to verify placement of an advertisement.
Audience: Readers for whom a magazine is written and edited. Also called target audience.
Audit: A verification of a magazine's circulation.
Bimonthly: A publication issued once every two months.
Biweekly: A publication issued once every two weeks.
Bleed: An extra amount of printed image that extends beyond the trim edge of the sheet of the page.
Bulk Copies: Copies or subscriptions purchased in quantities of five or more that promote the business or professional interest of the purchaser.
Business or B-to-B Publication: A publication that covers a specific industry, occupation or profession and is published to inform persons actively engaged in the field.

Cash Discount: A discount off the cost of advertising space for cash payment, usually 2% of the net.

Center Spread: The two facing center pages of a publication.

Classified Advertising: Type-driven advertising, usually with uniform type.

Close: The deadline by which an advertiser must reserve advertising space or send in advertising material for a given issue.

Complimentary (or Comp) Copy or Subscription: A free issue or subscription sent to an advertiser or advertising agency.

Cost-Per-Thousand: A standard measurement used by many advertising agencies to assess ad cost efficiency. To calculate cost-per-thousand (CPM), divide the advertising rate by the total circulation and then multiply by 1000.

Earned Rate: The rate an advertiser earns based on the advertiser's actual volume and frequency during a specified time period.

Frequency: The number of advertising insertions purchased during a specified period, generally a year. The more insertions an advertiser reserves, the greater the frequency discount.

Gatefold: A four-page sheet that is bound and creased so that it opens like a two-page spread.

Group Discount: A lower advertising rate earned by an advertiser when insertions are placed in a group of publications.

I.B.C.: The inside back cover of a magazine. Also called third cover or Cover III.

I.F.C.: The inside front cover of a magazine. Also called second cover or Cover II.

Insert: An advertising page that is supplied by

the advertiser for placement in a magazine Usually an advertiser-supplied insert is heavier than the paper the magazine is printed on.

Insertion Order: A written order from the advertiser or advertising agency to the magazine publisher to run a specified advertisement in a specified issue.

Island Position: Advertising on a page that is completely surrounded by editorial.

Make-Good: When a magazine refunds an advertiser with a free run of an advertisement due to an error in a previous issue.

Masthead: A listing of a magazine's staff and ownership, usually appearing on a page toward the front the magazine.

Merchandising: Any activity offered by the magazine publisher that enhances an advertiser's ad campaign. Merchandising can be in the form of list rentals, sweepstakes, event marketing, point-of-purchase displays, etc.

Net: The amount paid to the magazine publisher by the advertising agency or advertiser after deducting the agency commission.

One-time Rate: Advertising charge for a single insertion.

Open Rate: The basic rate for advertising, same as one-time.

Pass-along Audience: Persons other than the initial reader who read some part of the publication.

Preferred Position: Specified advertising placement in a magazine requested by the advertiser or advertising agency.

Premium Position: Special preferred advertising position generally sold at a higher rate.

Promotion Copies: Copies sent to prospective advertisers and their advertising agencies.

Publisher's Statement: Sworn statement of circulation and distribution data for a six-month period.

Quantity Discount: Price discount for volume purchase of advertising within a specified time period.

R.O.P. (Run Of Press) Advertising: The placement of an advertisement on any page or position at the discretion of the magazine publisher.

Rate Card: A card or sheet of paper showing advertising rates, unit advertising sizes, mechanical requirements, closing dates and a variety of other information for the advertiser or advertising agency.

Readership Survey: A research study of a magazine's readership offering all kinds of statistical information. This may range from household income and years of schooling to shopping habits and types of consumer products purchased.

Rebate: A refund to an advertiser or advertising agency because of reduced circulation. Usually in the form of a make-good.

Short Rate: When the advertiser does not use the agreed-upon inserts within a given time period, the magazine publisher charges the advertiser the difference in frequency discounts.

Split Run: When an advertiser runs two or more advertisements in the same issue, but in varying regional print runs of the magazine.

Spread: An advertisement designed to spread across two facing pages. Also known as a dou-

207

ble spread or double truck.

Tear Sheets: Pages torn or cut from a magazine that are used as proof of insertion of an advertisement.

Trade Publication: A magazine serving a highly defined business audience.

I

INDEX

211

Musical inserts, 97

217

T
Telephone marketing firms, 88
Time, 27, 38
Time, Inc., 53, 66
Trade magazines, 29–30, 114–116. *See also*
      Business-to-business magazines
  salaries in publishing, 50
Trademark, 126
Trade shows, 116–120
Type alignment, 79

V
Value-added program, 37
Vendors servicing magazine publisher, 85–90
Video and MultiMedia Producer, 116
Video Software Dealers Association Convention, 120
Video Systems, 116
Video technology, 112–114
Vogue, 38

W
Web page designers, 107–108
WEBTechniques, 116
Web.X-The Internet Event for Business, 120
Wenner, Jann, 28
Western Publications Association, 157–158
WYSIWYG (What You See Is What You Get)
      software, 109